Organizing Corporeal Ethics

T0347938

This book explores the meaning and practice of corporeal ethics in organized life. Corporeal ethics originates from an emergent, embodied, and affective experience with others that precedes and exceeds those rational schemes that seek to regulate it. Pullen and Rhodes show how corporeal ethics is fundamentally based in embodied affect, yet practically materialized in ethico-political acts of positive resistance and networked solidarity. Considering ethics in this way turns our attention to how people's conduct and interactions might be ethically informed in the context of, and in resistance to, the masculine rationality of dominating organizational power relations in which they find themselves. Pullen and Rhodes outline the ways in which ethically grounded resistance and critique can and do challenge self-interested organizational power and privilege. They account for how corporeal ethics serves to destabilize the ways that organizations reproduce practices that negate difference and result in oppression, discrimination, and inequality.

The book is suitable for students, scholars, and citizens who want to learn more about the radical possibilities of how political actions arising from corporeal ethics can strive for equality and justice.

Alison Pullen is Professor of Gender, Work and Organization at Macquarie University, Australia.

Carl Rhodes is Professor of Organization Studies at the University of Technology Sydney, Australia.

State of the Art in Business Research
Series Editor: Geoffrey Wood

Recent advances in theory, methods and applied knowledge (alongside structural changes in the global economic ecosystem) have presented researchers with challenges in seeking to stay abreast of their fields and navigate new scholarly terrains.

State of the Art in Business Research presents shortform books which provide an expert map to guide readers through new and rapidly evolving areas of research. Each title will provide an overview of the area, a guide to the key literature and theories and time-saving summaries of how theory interacts with practice.

As a collection, these books provide a library of theoretical and conceptual insights, and exposure to novel research tools and applied knowledge, that aid and facilitate in defining the state of the art, as a foundation stone for a new generation of research.

Organizing Corporeal Ethics
A Research Overview
Alison Pullen and Carl Rhodes

For more information about this series, please visit: www.routledge.com/State-of-the-Art-in-Business-Research/book-series/START

Organizing Corporeal Ethics

A Research Overview

Alison Pullen and Carl Rhodes

Routledge
Taylor & Francis Group

LONDON AND NEW YORK

First published 2022
by Routledge
2 Park Square, Milton Park, Abingdon, Oxon OX14 4RN

and by Routledge
605 Third Avenue, New York, NY 10158

Routledge is an imprint of the Taylor & Francis Group, an informa business

British Library Cataloguing-in-Publication Data
A catalogue record for this book is available from the British Library

Library of Congress Cataloging-in-Publication Data
A catalog record has been requested for this book

ISBN: 978-0-367-89881-6 (hbk)
ISBN: 978-1-032-16955-2 (pbk)
ISBN: 978-1-003-03104-8 (ebk)

DOI: 10.4324/9781003031048

Typeset in Times New Roman
by codeMantra

Contents

Preface

This book was completed from our Sydney home, a home which sits on the lands of the Gadigal people of the Eora nation. The Gadigal people are the first peoples and the traditional custodians of these lands; lands for which they never ceded sovereignty to the European colonizers. The word Eora means 'here' or 'from this place', and the Eora nation comprises the people of what is now referred to as the Sydney coastal region (Heiss and Gibson, 2020). As foreigners, we recognize that we live on land that does not belong to us. We acknowledge that by being here, we have a responsibility to care for the land, a land that cares for us. As first-generation immigrants to this country, we have a personal connection to the land on which we are guests of the Gadigal people. This land is where Alison gave birth to our son Elliot 13 years ago, and where Carl's older children James, Daniel, and Natalie became adults. This is a land of struggle born of colonial invasion, and one where reconciliation between Indigenous and non-Indigenous Australian people has still not been achieved, albeit long overdue.

The ideas housed in this book are the product of discussions that we have had for 15 years, a time of deep personal and intellectual connection between us. This is also a time during which we have raised our son. When we started to write together, and as reiterations of text emerged between us, we were no longer able to see where Carl and Alison started and ended. At times it feels as though we are talking to each other. At other times it feels like we can speak in one voice. Speech of that kind comes from openness, trust, and respect for the words of each other. They manifest in texts written in the good times and the bad times. When relationships are strained, collective words mark a search for the creative out of the fruitless.

Writing has become a means to connect and reconnect. In some ways, our work on embodiment and ethics is a process through which we acknowledge that the other, no matter how close, cannot be fully known. The other can never be successfully reduced to being a possession of one's own categories of knowledge. Our writing surfaces elements of knowing ourselves and each other, but this is partial, fragmented, and vulnerable. Writing this book, which is based on work we have done together over the past decade, was an occasion for reflection on the life we built together, on how we see ourselves, as well as on how we see our family, friends, and colleagues.

We have benefited from generous, open reciprocal relationships with so many people. The ideas in this book emerged from our interactions with others, both known and the unknown. We are the conduits of ideas that precede us, and that at best we leave some small mark on as they pass through our bodies. When Alison types, she sees the back of her hand and her mother appears. As Carl reads Alison's words, he remembers a book he read in high school. The ideas we sometimes dare call our own arise inter-generationally. Even when we depart from our ancestors, both familial and intellectual, they live materially through and on our skin. They re-emerge in our texts, despite ourselves. Our ideas also manifest through our lives together and the everyday moments we share. These experiences, while more often than not mundane, are also not separable from the realities of our social existence as privileged academics of European origin, a decidedly middle-class position no matter what one's upbringing. Neither are our experiences separable from the gendered, raced, and classed genealogies of our lives. Knowledge can be challenging and rewarding. Sometimes it surfaces in words between us. Other times speech fails. Maybe it is during these failures that we learn the most about each other. The ability to catch our eyes at the same time, to pause, and to be. Silent. Together. Body with body. Decisions that emerge from trials, from these embodied relations where speech fails us, always feel right regardless of the risks attached and the levels of the unknown.

Our son Elliot has taught us much about corporeal ethics, starting as baby when he could not speak, of course, but could still relate and receive care. Rationality and language are not primary in relationships. Elliot showed us the importance of being able to act before thought, as well as how to be responsible for someone entirely dependent for the continuation of life. It is a child who can teach the importance of trust, care, and love in unequal relationships. He is now teaching us to listen and respect difference. There are significant inter-generational challenges for young Australians, especially those like Elliot who benefit from Australia's colonial past. The environments in which they are nurtured are important for fostering productive and ethical relationships and attending to conflicts both past and present. These are ideas very much connected to this book, a book that is concerned with the ways knowing and unknowing, body and mind, ethics and justice, and self and other become intertwined in the pursuit of ethics in organizations. Corporeality – a down to earth attention to the lived body that is experienced in relation to others is emphasized. The body, the corpus, is the material form through which we live, think, and feel. Corporeality is the physical and material reality with which relations between people are forged in local contexts, in the book's case in organizations. It is easy to take the body for granted, at least when it is in good working order and not in pain, focusing instead on more lofty thoughts, ideas, or even spiritual musings. By corollary, writing about the body and of the possibility of corporeal ethics is fraught, as the words we use are necessarily extracted from feeling and bodily motion. At times we take the body for granted, even as we speak and write about it, only to be reminded by a pang of hunger, a flush of embarrassment the creaking pain of an old joint, memories of being cut open or when trauma presents viscerally. Often, we can take the body for granted by abstracting it as a universal idea, a human experience that transcends the body's sex, colour, or ability. We are not immune to such habits. However, we remind ourselves that corporeality is the basis for relations to others, including those in organizations. Those relations are where our attention is directed, in different ways, in the chapters of this book.

We completed *Organizing Corporeal Ethics* in 2021, a year which saw the world experience the COVID-19 pandemic. The year 2021 was full of global challenges differentially experienced in different nations and by different people. For many, this was devastating as death tolls mounted, and people lost their means of maintaining their livelihoods. For those of us fortunate to live in countries which responded quickly with virus control and health management, the pandemic still challenged the capabilities of humans to be resilient. For those less fortunate, the consequences have been more severe as people in their millions became sick and died.

The pandemic cannot be separated from the destruction of the planet at the hands of industrial capitalism, excess consumer consumption, and corporate greed and corruption. Nor can it be separated from the resurgent horrors of populist far-right governments and associated patriarchal leadership infused with toxic masculinity of the worst kind. In the 20th Anniversary preface of *Talkin' up to the White Woman* (2020), Aileen Moreton-Robinson offers the following wisdom on COVID-19:

> Those of us who survive are left to deal with loss, grief and fear. We are facing an invisible enemy that socially and physically isolates

the living and the dead. A virus that has debilitated economies in the space of a few months. Biology has confounded politics and economies reminding us of our vulnerability as a species. Social distancing provides the only sense of reassurance that mediates the fraught, painful and difficult situation humans face at this moment in history. A moment we share with mother earth who is showing signs of recovery across land, sea, water, and air. Global noise and pollution reduction in the ocean and land has allowed our non-human relatives to reap the benefits of human containment and inactivity. Birds are chirping, whales are singing, and mother earth is recuperating, My hope is that the significance of this moment speaks to and is understood by humans, but I fear any introspection gained will be lost once the virus subsides. Power too is infectious and spreads like a virus fed by human dominance and superiority.

On the one hand, the virus has exposed the hubris of human power as the world succumbed to a virus that exposed the vulnerability of the human body. On the other hand, it showed that the dominance of particular power relations in capitalist societies means that people do not experience this vulnerability equally. In the United Kingdom, the Institute for Fiscal Studies found that minority ethnic groups were at significantly higher risk from COVID-19. For Black Caribbean people living in the United Kingdom, for example, the mortality rate was three times higher than the British majority (Platt and Warwick, 2020). As in many other parts of the world, in Australia, COVID-19 resulted in rising levels of unemployment, homelessness, and domestic violence against women. In some parts of the country, the instance of domestic violence increased by more than 40% (Equity Economics, 2020).

Nadje Al-Ali (2020), speaking on the effects of the pandemic in the Global South on women, writes that specific risks and vulnerabilities are associated with intersectional inequalities well entrenched before COVID-19. Al-Ali highlights how COVID-19 has exacerbated the challenges of poverty and lack of adequate health care faced by LGBTQ people, ethnic minorities, domestic workers, migrants, and sex workers. Like Nadia Al-Ali, Banu Özkazanç-Pan and Alison Pullen (2021) call for recognizing women's labour in the plans for economic recovery which need to start by acknowledging that women have been disproportionately affected by the pandemic. Women are at significant risk from increased unemployment and precarious work. They do more formal care work in aged and health care and do more unpaid domestic labour. Women are also often the care workers for children, the sick and elderly, and do unpaid work in the community.

As Tithi Bhattacharya (in Jaffe, 2020) explains, the pandemic has proven to us, as if it was not apparent before, just how vital care work is to society. It has also shown us, she argues, how hopeless capitalism is at supporting embodied human life, even in the wealthiest nations. This is especially so in the United States where universal health care has so wantonly been resisted in favour of a user-pays capitalist model, that too many people can simply not afford. COVID-19 has shone a light on the problems of inequality and discrimination inherent in the global economic system, a system where poverty, lack of health care, unaffordable housing, and climate catastrophe are central features (Arruzza et al., 2019). Australia is a case in point, where First Nations Australians are at unique risk from COVID-19 due to social, economic, and health inequalities. In remote areas of the country, this is even worse, due to 'marginalization from health services, food insecurity, and poor access to water, sanitation, and adequate housing that accommodates larger family groups' (Yashadhana et al., 2020: n.p.).

The pandemic has returned the world's attention to the body in a way that we could not have imagined when we started the work that is enclosed in the present volume. The corporeal ethics that we explore here – an ethics of caring and generous relations between embodied human beings – is perhaps now more relevant than ever. As well as COVID-19, the current juncture of history is one where the body is politicized in particular ways. At unprecedented levels, people around the work are taking to the streets to mobilize injustice rendered on specific bodies. Pro-choice rallies demand that women's bodies are no longer under control of patriarchal legislators who would seek to limit women's reproductive rights and self-determination. Around the world, people have marched against and again to assert that Black Lives Matter, despite the scourge of racialized incarceration, deaths in custody, and police violence against Black people.

Since 2017 women across the globe have taken to the streets annually to protest sexism and misogyny, many wearing knitted 'pussy hats' in rebuke of Donald Trump having fecklessly bragged that his celebrity to grab women 'by the pussy' whenever he wishes. The Extinction Rebellion has occupied public space in the United Kingdom, the United States, Canada, and Australia to protest the 'social and ecological collapse' and 'mass extinction' caused by climate change. In all cases, it is the assembly of human bodies, and the relation between those bodies, that has been the means through which an ethically motivated democratic politics has been mobilized (see Butler, 2015). This is a democracy where oppression of particular 'types' of bodies is contested and their continued capacity for existence is pursued by real people working together in proximity.

On a more prosaic level, the pandemic has required individuals to rethink their everyday interactions with others. Social distancing has surfaced fear between people and in some cases, a fear of people. Meanwhile, the face mask has become a politically divisive symbol. For some, it is a restriction of personal freedom, such that wearing a mask indicates a lack of self-determination, or even a sign of weakness. It is such rampant selfish individualism that disavows the kind of ethics we are concerned with, ethics whose direction is to the care of well-being of others. Amidst all of this, we retain hope that the fundamental act of caring for other people in the context of material and embodied relations can still animate human life. Through such animation, ethics becomes translated into politics – politics that demands that we care for each other more. This politics can arise through activism, through assembly, and through democratic participation, as we saw in the examples above. It can also occur in workplaces and organizations as people strive together for better lives, and struggle against oppression, inequality, and injustice. It is to better understand this struggle that we hope this book contributes.

References

Arruzza, C., Bhattacharya, T., and Fraser, N. (2019) *Feminism for the 99%: A Manifesto*. London: Verso.

Butler, J. (2015) *Notes towards a Performative Theory of Assembly*. Cambridge, MA: Harvard University Press.

Equity Economics. (2020) *A Wave of Disadvantage across NSW: Impact of the Covid-19 Recession*. A Report Prepared for the New South Wales Council of Social Service, Sydney.

Heiss, A., and Gibson, M.-J. (2020) Aboriginal people and place, *Barani: Sydney's Aboriginal History*, Sydney; Barani. Online, accessed 20 November 2020: https://www.sydneybarani.com.au/sites/aboriginal-people-and-place/

Moreton-Robinson, A. (2020) *Talkin' Up to the White Woman: Indigenous Women and Feminism, 20th Anniversary Edition*. Brisbane: University of Queensland Press.

Özkazanç-Pan, B., and Pullen, A. (2021, in press) Reimagining value: A feminist commentary in the midst of the Covid-19 pandemic. *Gender, Work and Organization*. https://doi.org/10.1111/gwao.12591

Platt, L., and Warwick, R. (2020) *Are Some Ethnic Groups More Vulnerable to COVID-19 than Others?* London: The Institute for Fiscal Studies.

Yashadhana, A., Pollard-Wharton, N., Zwi, A., and Biles, B. (2020) Indigenous Australians at increased risk of COVID-19 due to existing health and socioeconomic inequities. *The Lancet Regional Health – Western Pacific*. Online: https://doi.org/10.1016/j.lanwpc.2020.100007

Acknowledgements

We acknowledge the Wattamattagal clan of the Darug nation and the Gadigal people of the Eora Nation on whose unceded lands our respective Universities (Macquarie University and the University of Technology Sydney) are located. We recognize them as the traditional custodians of knowledge for these lands and pay our respects to their Ancestors and their Elders.

Corporeal Ethics and Organization is the culmination of work we have been doing together over the past ten years. It has benefited from insights and commentary in many scholarly meetings, both personal and institutional. We have especially valued the opportunity to present this work at forums convened by the European Group on Organization Studies (EGOS), the International Conference in Critical Management Studies, and the conference of the journal *Gender, Work and Organization*. Alison had the privilege to present a PhD course on Corporeal Ethics at the University of Lapland and thank the generosity of relations.

Earlier versions of ideas presented here have been published in the journals *Organization* and *International Journal of Management Reviews*, and we thank those journals for giving us permission to develop that work in this volume. Chapters 1, 2, and 4 draw on and develop Pullen, A., and Rhodes, C. (2014) Corporeal ethics and the politics of resistance in organizations. *Organization*, 21(6): 782–796, and Pullen, A., and Rhodes, C. (2015) Ethics, embodiment and organizations. *Organization*, 22(2): 159–165. Chapter 3 extends from Rhodes, C., and Pullen, A. (2018) Critical business ethics: From corporate self-interest to the glorification of the sovereign pater. *International Journal of Management Reviews*, 20(2): 483–499.

Sincere thanks to Terry Clague's long-standing support and to Adam Woods for his editorial guidance.

Elliot, Natalie, Daniel, and James we appreciate you; thanks for challenging our taken-for-granted assumptions and for showing us new ways of relating. To Ted and Rupert thanks for keeping life simple.

1 The ethics of organization

Over the past 20 years, ethics has become a central theme in the study of organizations, widely recognized as a 'growing and important field of study' (McLeod et al., 2016: 430). Often fuelled by a sense of moral outrage over the corporate scandals that elevated the ethics of business to the centre of the public stage, researchers have questioned the morality of business, especially as it relates to the exercise of increasingly vast corporate power on an international scale (Pullen and Rhodes, 2015a). In response, there have been various demands for a new and different type of ethics that might better respond to the inequalities produced by contemporary global capitalism (Rhodes, 2019) in a manner that enacts non-violent ethics of relations between people at work (Tyler, 2019).

In terms of these interpersonal relations, the 'ethics of organization' (Phillips and Margolis, 1999; Hancock, 2008) or 'organizational ethics' (Sims, 1991; Barker, 2002) attends to how ethics can be brought to bear on the complex institutional contexts in which members of organizations find themselves. This reflects a distinction between the general remit of business ethics, and the specific organizational focus of an ethics of organizations. As a field of study and practice, business ethics corals a wide set of concerns as related to 'the morals of commercial and corporate conduct' (Heath et al., 2018: 1). On the basis of such encompassing definitions, phenomena researched in business ethics include, inter alia, corporate social responsibility, environmental sustainability, economic crises, modern slavery, globalization, corporate governance, marketing, accounting, and finance.

When it comes to an ethics of organization, the focus is directed explicitly at how ethics relates to the management and organization of work as manifest in the political, social, and interpersonal relationships between people in organizations, as well as their institutionalization. Of concern is the way that people might collectively mobilize

DOI: 10.4324/9781003031048-1

and organize to realize ethically motivated political projects. Consequently, the study of the ethics of organization has been dominated by the question of what form of ethics, either normative or descriptive, might be appropriate for the characteristics of organizational life that are distinct from other ethical domains. This begins with a doubt that ethical theory developed in relation to other substantive spheres of life can simply be 'applied' to organizations without 7.

The ethics of organization has drawn attention to what organizations might do to develop 'objectives and practices which are morally legitimate' (Wicks and Freeman, 1998: 128). Established concerns centre on how organizations can achieve improved levels of ethicality (e.g. Phillips and Margolis, 1999; Hancock, 2008; Constantinescu and Kaptein, 2020), as well as on criticizing organizations for their ethical inadequacies and failures (e.g. Roberts, 2001; Jones, 2003; Rhodes, 2016). More recent writing has directed attention to the ethics at play in organizations despite, rather than because of, an organization's managerially sanctioned or administered ethical arrangements (e.g. Munro, 2014; Rhodes, 2016). Further, while resistance to organizational power and control has been a long-standing topic of study (e.g. Jermier et al., 1994; Fleming and Spicer, 2003; Westwood and Johnston, 2012; Mc-Cabe, 2019) if and how ethics can be played out in the form of such resistance has also begun to be explored (e.g. Helin and Sandström, 2010; McMurray et al., 2011; Knights, 2015; Rhodes et al., 2020).

With this book, we follow the trajectory of the approach to the ethics of organization that does not privilege management and managerialism as the locus of power or central point of inquiry. Indeed, such a privileging is part of a long-established practice of gendered organizations that privilege masculine organizational norm (Acker, 1990; Knights and Pullen, 2019) as characterized by instrumental rationality, hierarchy, and sovereignty. Thirty years ago, Joan Acker elaborated that organizations are structured around gender differences that privilege the masculine in a way that suppresses femininity as being emotional and outside of the realm of rational organization. In such organizational contexts, ethics too can be subject to an un-named masculinity based on reciprocity of exchange, calculation of self-advantage, and rationalization. What Acker called the gendered organization is not simply a matter of structures, plans, and representational hierarchies. It is a context in which people live their lives, and through which those lives can be affected by the gendered, raced, classed, and sexualized structures (Acker, 2006; Britton and Logan, 2008) as they are experienced in affective intercorporeal interaction with others (Pullen et al., 2017). Feminist research has been the location of much critique of gendered inequality in organizations, offering insight into how resistance manifests and how ethics emerge from resistance (Fotaki et al., 2014; Kenny and Fotaki, 2015; Vachhani and Pullen, 2019). The corporeal ethics of organization we address in this book seeks to redress rationalization of ethics through an ethics that is:

> crucially concerned with the specificity of one's embodiment [... and...] is prior to the conceptualization of ethics as reducible to a set of universal principles dictated by reason (whose reason?). It is opposed to any system of ethics which elevates itself from a contingent form of life to the pretension of being the *one* necessary form of life.
>
> (Grosz, 1994: 26)

Rather than being universal, corporeal ethics is the domain of the 'embodied ethical human being-in-the-world', suffused by affect, intimacy, and the non-rational (McCarthy, 2010: 3). That by Western standards these categories are culturally feminine is part and parcel of their neglect in the masculine gendered organization. This critique has issued a call that:

> a new ethico-political ideal is required to contest the adequacy of dominant understandings of social interaction as matters of choice and rational decision-making and in contesting these understandings encourage us to imagine social alternatives.
>
> (Beasley and Bacchi, 2007: 1464)

For us, corporeal ethics offers such an alternative, in particular an alternative to the commonly rationalized ethics that we find dominant in both the theory and practice of organizations. Corporeal ethics turns our attention to how people's conduct and interaction in organizations might be ethically informed in the context of, and in resistance to, the masculine rationality of dominating organizational power relations in which they find themselves. This includes power relations that would seek to render ethics itself in a rational-masculine form.

Although gender is central to corporeal ethics, it is by far not the sole basis of difference that matters. Indeed, it calls 'calls attention to the causal forces marking, empowering, or depleting some bodies' (Sharp, 2019: 799), whether that force is applied idiosyncratically, or on account of the, among other things, sexed, racialized, gendered, classed nature of those bodies. Ethics comes to the fore in resistance to forms of oppression to which some bodies are subjected. However, this is not a form of resistance that is born simply out of an antipathy towards authority as a matter of principle or a negative oppositional desire. It is resistance motivated by care and concern arising when the well-being of others is damaged by the way that work is organized.

In articulating corporeal ethics, we are centrally informed by how feminist scholars have approached and theorized embodiment and ethics (Grosz, 1994; Gatens, 1996; Diprose, 2002; Shildrick, 2015). Reflecting on the ethics that emerge intercorporeally, we consider ethics as emerging from openness and generosity towards other people as it occurs in organizations. This is a form of hospitality in which the other person is given priority over the self as one is called to responsibility for that other person (Diprose, 1994, 2002, 2013). Relating this ethics to organizational life is not about the institutionalization of a set of conditions that aver that they can promote or ensure ethical behaviour among members of an organization (Weber, 1993). To do so would conflate ethics with the rational imposition of one person's will over another. Corporeal ethics originates from an emergent, embodied and affective experience with others that precedes and exceeds those rational schemes that seek to regulate it; an experience that 'constitutes social relations [...] and communal existence' (Diprose, 2002: 5).

To think of generosity this way positions it:

> not as a regulative ideal, but as a constitutive practice of sociality, community, and being together. It is in this sense [...] that generosity be thought of as a modality of power [...] is a practice through which people ordinarily act in concert to sustain relationships over time and space, relationships that enact their own normative principles and which depend upon non-sovereign modes of selfhood [...] generosity is not a 'moral' concept at all, in so far as this is meant to imply a regulative ideal of some sort against which the actualities of practice can be judged and evaluated from the position of an impartial observer.
>
> (Barnett and Land, 2007: 1073)

To develop an understanding of this communal and affectively charged ethics, the book examines 'embodied ethics' (Gatens, 1996) and 'corporeal generosity' (Diprose, 2002), considering how a specifically relational and embodied approach might inform an ethics of organization (cf. Roberts, 2001; Hancock, 2008). We explore the ethical relations that are marked affectively by generosity; a generosity based on acceptance and welcome of other people's difference. Such generosity can materialize in political acts that interrupt and disturb those practices of organizational power that work to close down difference. This political actualization is realized in the form of an ethico-politics of resistance that is not so much about passing judgements as it is about disrupting the taken-for-granted means through which judgement is violently and rationally imposed.

Our central purpose is to articulate an ethics of organization that is embodied and pre-reflective in origin, and socio-political in practice. Such ethics manifests in resisting those forms of organizing that close down difference and enact oppression; a practice we refer to as an ethico-politics of resistance. Through the course of the book, we show how the uptake of ethical openness and generosity is a matter of resisting those practices of organizing that deny or oppress difference and/or privilege certain modes of identity; examples of this being sexism, racism, violence, and the inequitable distribution of wealth (Dunne et al., 2008; Vachhani and Pullen, 2019). Corporeal ethics is an especially valuable approach to understanding and informing ethics in organizations when it results in contesting such practices. This approach avers the power and potential of each person and their body, and how that can move beyond self-interested identity politics towards a politics of the collective.

In bringing this ethics to the fore, we are by no means suggesting that the ideas and practices we present constitute some form of normative totalization that would supersede how others have conceived of an ethics of organization. There is a particular tendency in academic writing that privileges argumentation inscribed in 'masterful, rational and penetrating masculine forms' (Pullen and Rhodes, 2015b: 87). Central to such writing is an imagining that theorizing is a form of Darwinian competition by which one should present one's ideas through a rhetoric that imagines that they will overcome the shortcomings of that which has come before. In this model, ideas have to fight it out for supremacy in a somewhat pathetically imagined battle to be king of the (intellectual) playground. Hopefully, we do not participate in such modes of thinking or writing: modes that reflect a masculine desire for domination and supremacy. If such writing 'consumes the other through authoritative statements which offer closure and completeness' (Phillips et al., 2014: 323), we wish to resist this by offering an approach to the ethics of organizations that is additive and engaged. We acknowledge too that masculine desire seductively works through academic writing and leaves traces that defy intent. While we have not written this book in a deliberatively experimental feminine fashion (see Pullen, 2018), we have tried to be reflexive in the gendered character of our writing and thinking so as to offer the book as a means through which to attend to dimensions of ethics that are just beginning to be explored by organizational scholars. In this regard, we join De Coster is calling for a relational ethics that frees itself from 'normative business ethics of exchange', and hopes that an 'unburdened ethical female subjectivity can emerge' (2020: 751).

The ethics we write about is enacted by and through living human bodies that are relationally entwined with others' bodies (Pullen et al., 2017). We maintain that this corporeal ethics constitutes an emerging and important approach to the ethics of organization. It does so by attending to how ethics is grounded in an embodied experience that occurs before rational calculation and responds openly and generously to the needs of others (see Diprose, 2002; Kenny and Fotaki, 2015; Pullen and Rhodes, 2015c; De Coster, 2020) through the interpersonal and collective interaction and movement of bodies (Butler, 2015; Tyler, 2019). In organizations, such an ethics manifests in social relations that both resist power's tendency to domination and encourages the possibility of free, reciprocal, and joyous encounters (see also Thanem and Wallenberg, 2015) between people. Beyond formal organizations it manifests in the organization of affective relations in the pursuit of justice and equality.

An ethics for organizations?

In the next chapter, we explore in more detail what we mean by a corporeal ethics of organization. Before moving on to that, however, it is important to situate this among broader discussions and theorizations of organizational ethics. The question of organizational ethics has been the subject of much discussion since the late 1970s. In its inception, the focus was on institutionalizing ethics within organizations through employee commitment to norms understood as ethical (Sims, 1991). It was argued that ethicality could be achieved through leadership, corporate culture, top management support (Jose and Thibodeaux, 1999), creating formal positions responsible for ethics, and implementing codes of ethics (Vitell and Singhapakdi, 2008). Commitment to ethical norms was to be ensured through organizational leaders' transformational capacities (Carlson and Perrewe, 1995) that would enable value systems to be embedded in an organization's culture (Nicotera and Cushman, 1992). Countering the possibility that socialization into organizations, environmental influences, and hierarchal modes of organizing might inhibit organizational ethics, researchers examined the ways that organizations could arrange themselves to yield 'higher levels of ethical behaviour' (Smith and Carroll, 1984: 95; see also Metzger et al., 1993).

The normative position was stated unambiguously by Boling (1978) as: '[a]n organization should establish its own conduct standards, systematize its ethical obligations into clear, concise statements, and socialize its members toward understanding and conformity' (p. 360). The three explicit bases of organizational ethics as expounded by Boling were that: (1) organizations should establish explicit ethical premises; (2) individual moral judgements in organizations should be based on the norms of the group; and (3) ethics must be realized through cooperative social relations. Focusing on management's responsibility to develop and implement mechanisms that direct and control employees' ethical behaviour became somewhat of a default position in organizational ethics. This is indicative of a strong and established trend that focuses on how managers have responsibility for 'sustaining ethics in their organizations' (McDaniel, 2001: 1) with 'individual employees and groups of employees hav[ing] a responsibility to behave according to the norms and values of the organization' (Verkerk et al., 2001: 354).

Although interest in organizational ethics was growing within the business ethics literature, since the late 1990s these concerns have been brought to bear on mainstream organization studies. A key turning point was a paper by Wicks and Freeman in 1998 in which the authors claimed that 'organization studies needs to be fundamentally reshaped [...] to provide room for ethics' (p. 123). They argued that discussions of ethics were relatively absent in organization studies at that time and had led to an ethical naiveté among organizational researchers who were operating through a set of non-explicit and under-developed ethical positions. When ethics did come into play, it was something 'tacked on' to research post-hoc and not centrally incorporated into the research.

Since Wicks and Freeman's article's publication, there has been substantial growth in research and theorizing into organizational ethics, both within the business ethics and organizations studies literatures. Responding to the fact that 'business ethics as a field [had] only partially grasped the significance of organizations' (Phillips and Margolis, 1999: 620) the ethics of organization moved beyond straightforward managerial normativism of earlier approaches (e.g. Boling, 1978; Smith and Carrol, 1984; Sims, 1991) towards developing unique models and theories of ethics that are specific to the context of organizations. Organization studies scholars have worked towards various conceptions of 'an ethics of organization' (Phillips and Margolis, 1999; Hancock, 2008) or an 'organizational ethics' (Sims, 1991; Barker, 2002) that is 'tailored to the defining problems of corporate morality' (Wempe, 2008: 1337).

The idea of organizational ethics responds to the question of how ethics is practised and institutionalized between people in organizations in terms of how organizations might guide, influence, or control such practice. On this basis, it has been argued that 'organizations need an ethics of their own, distinct from political theory and moral philosophy' (Phillips and Margolis, 1999: 619). Moreover, the development of this ethics would 'put ethicists in the business of specifying and justifying substantive aims for organizations, their owners, and their managers to pursue' (p. 630). Such an ethics attends to 'determining the justifiability of organizational arrangements' (p. 631) while at the same time ensuring that ethics can be 'kept alive in organizations' (p. 633). While the assumed need for a unique ethics for organizations was questioned from the outset (Hartman, 2001) the subsequent development of the ethics of organizations has been much less focused and singular than Phillips and Margolis' call to arms wished for. Amidst this, one of the most vital areas of inquiry has concentrated less on how organizations can effectively manage ethics, and more on the ways such forms of management might inhibit ethical behaviour.

In a study of the ethics of organizational downsizing Rhodes et al. (2010) suggest that dominant cultural norms in organizations diminish 'the capacity for organizations to scrutinize the ethics of their actions' (p. 535); in their case when downsizing comes to be viewed a standard business practice. This is so because ethics requires questioning preconceived ideas and institutionalized norms and that strong cultures where such ideas and norms are taken for granted prevent this questioning from occurring. In another study, Helin and Sandstrom (2010) examined the implementation of a code of conduct ostensibly designed for the purpose of securing organizational ethics. However, they found that even though the members of the organization felt compelled to sign up to the code formally, they largely rejected it both morally and practically. This case demonstrated how, ironically, the implementation of organizational ethics 'had a rather negative impact on the ethical climate in the organization' (p. 599).

These examples contrast the ethics that are embedded in the micro-practices of everyday organizational life with those that focus on macro-institutional forces thought to guide ethics. Gordon et al. (2009) explored this in a study of the police force in the Australian state of New South Wales. The authors found was that public and organizational pressure for reform to address corruption in the Force served to 'undermine the objective of a more ethically sound organization' (p. 93) by inadvertently reinforcing already established power relations. Besides formal organizational programmes, researchers have also attended to how inexplicit and culturally embedded forms of ethics can limit the ethical possibilities of organization. Bell et al. (2012) also examine the limitations of managerially imposed organizational ethics by interrogating how ingrained religious concepts can inform executive action, focusing on organizational spirituality, as popularized as a corporate practice in 'belief-led' businesses primarily in the United States. Central to this form of organizing is the idea that organizations can be thought of as having 'souls'. In criticizing the workplace spirituality movement, Bell, Taylor and Driscoll argue that promoting the idea of a corporation as having a 'healthy-minded organizational soul restricts ethical reflection through systematic exclusion of even the possibility of unethical or damaging activities' (p. 434). In place, they advocate for a more critical approach to ethics that would emerge through an 'ethical skepticism concerning the nature of organizational activities' (p. 425) so as to combat the inevitability of ethically questionable organizational behaviour. By this account, an ethics of organization can only be pursued if the organization is prepared to confront the presence of harm that can occur within them.

These studies suggest that the practice of ethics is situated in organizational culture and tradition, most especially the rules and norms within or against which ethics is enacted individually (Clegg et al., 2007), such that ethics cannot be determined by managerial will, fiat, or programme. This situatedness infers that although normalizing organizational ethics that posit what it means to be an 'ideal type' of employee can be found in organizations, this does not determine the subjectivity of each employee (Rhodes et al., 2010). It acts a strong force, but one that can nevertheless be relativized or resisted through alternatives and micro-discourses (Meriläinen et al., 2004), which can also be explicitly ethical. Individual identity in organizations is thus a site of struggle (Thomas and Linstead, 2002); one where at least it is possible to find 'a balance between a sense of ethical selfhood and dominant organizational discourse' (Poldner et al., 2019). It is thus possible for a person's ethical impulses to be stirred by a mistrust of organizational ethics as being beholden to a legislative, authoritative (Wray-Bliss, 2009) and calculative impetus (Jones, 2003) that exerts pressure 'against moral agency' (Nielsen, 2006: 317). The ethics of organization that emerges is quite different from early calls for a normative managerially enforced ethics. This new approach advocates for the possibilities of how people might innovatively respond to such pressure, whether it be, for example, through individual ethical creativity (Bigo, 2018), or by publicly holding organizations to account for their actions (Rhodes, 2016).

As we have seen in the discussions of organizational ethics canvassed above, what might constitute such an ethics is considerably varied. This variation is not only in the theoretical approach and ethical theories employed. It is also in relation to whether researchers are advocating a particular means through which organizations can seek ethicality or whether they are providing a critique of how those means are implemented or responded to. However, common to these advocacy and critical approaches is a focus on what organizations should do or actually do to manage ethics. Contributions demonstrate that the main attention of organizational ethics has been on the ethical agency of organizations themselves, in terms of either valorizing it as the route to ethics, or condemning it as needing to be politically resisted. While this can be regarded as a significant development in a field not so long ago noted for the absence of ethical theorizing (Wicks and Freeman, 1998), it also indicates that how ethics might emerge from outside the managerial sub-class in organizations is an increasingly important area of study (e.g. Iedema and Rhodes, 2010; Munro, 2014; Fatien Diochon et al., 2018). There remains, however, a danger that the direction in which organizational ethics has developed is still dominated by the assumption that non-managerial members of organizations are inadvertently regarded only as the targets of organizational programmes, with the possibilities for their own active ethics left unaddressed. This suggests the need to 'unsettle organizational morality' (Weiskopf and Willmott, 2013) in both theory and practice.

Overview of the book

With the notion of corporeal ethics, this book further examines and theorizes a form of ethics of organization that is enacted outside of the agency of the formal power and authority. This ethics is located beyond any individual's identity and agency, arriving instead at the level of the embodied relations between people. We focus on embodied and relational interactions as the location at which ethics is both originated and enacted. In other words, ethics emerge through intercorporeality. In Chapter 2, 'Corporeal ethics and organizations', the book's central concept of corporeal ethics in organizations is developed and canvassed. Drawing on extant studies on the affective and embodied character of ethics, and ideas from feminist theory and phenomenological ethics, the chapter considers ethics as grounded in lived organizational experience between real embodied people. The embodied ethical encounter is conceived in terms of a generosity that both comes before and goes beyond self-interest, reciprocal calculation, and moral righteousness. In organizations, corporeal ethics is expanded in relation to the ethical demand to disrupt systems of normalization that attempt to close down difference.

The gendered character of corporeal ethics is discussed in Chapter 3, 'Ethics beyond organizational patriarchy'. Here we consider how the distinction between a corporeal and rational ethics is one that is primarily gendered; it is based on the long-standing association of the rational with the masculine and the affective with the feminine. The chapter explores how organizations can use a masculine conception of corporate ethics as a subterfuge for commercial self-interest. With corporate ethics our attention turns not to models or theories of ethics, but to what organizations actually do in the name of ethics and responsibility. We show how this practice can enact an unacknowledged patriarchy that associates ethics with traditionally masculine values of domination, greatness, and sovereignty. By contrast, corporeal ethics is further developed as a form of affective generosity that displaces patriarchal privilege in favour of the ongoing pursuit of care and nurturing of others and the elimination of human relations of domination.

Chapter 4, 'An ethico-politics of resistance', explores how corporeal ethics can practically manifest in organizations. The chapter concentrates on resistance as a lived response to demand of ethics, including the ways that dominant approaches to organizational ethics can inadvertently stymie this resistance. This emerges in what we refer to as an 'ethico-politics of resistance' that disrupts the taken-for-granted means through which moral judgement is imposed in and by organizations. We go on to consider how such disruption provides an antidote to normalization and to the social inequalities that it (re)produces. This shows how ethics is a productive form of embodied interactions that counters embedded habits of selfishness and fear of alterity.

The book concludes with Chapter 5, 'The affective organization of corporeal ethics'. This chapter focuses on the ethics that are enacted through the collective mobilization of bodies in actual, virtual, and transnational spaces. Our focus here is specifically on the organization of corporeal ethics as it occurs through political assembly and networked forms of solidarity. The neoliberalism which has seen the domination of corporate capitalism on a global scale has produced new forms of inequality and domination. It is also the site to new forms of organized resistance through social movements such as #McToo and Black Lives Matter. We suggest that corporeal ethics helps understand the efficacy and necessity of these movements as they continue to strive for justice and equality across the world.

Collectively these chapters explore corporeal ethics as it relates to the celebration of difference and being positively moved by intercorporeal relations with others. This is not an ethics that makes guarantees for righteousness or appeases ethical anxiety, but rather one that embraces human interaction in all of its ambiguity and complexity. Corporeal ethics in organizations is positioned as a horizon that calls one towards it, yet at which one never fully arrives. It is embarking on such a perilous but necessary journey that is required if ethics is to remain alive in the lives of people who encounter each other in organizations.

Our purpose in writing this book is to engage in the study of the ethics of organization by reviewing and extending existing research related to corporeal ethics. By exploring this growing and important approach to organizational ethics, we consider how corporeal ethics serves to destabilize the ways that organizations can reproduce practices that negate difference and result in oppression, discrimination, and inequality. In allowing for the importance of corporeal ethics for organizations, the book outlines how forms of ethically grounded resistance and critique can and do challenge self-interested organizational power and privilege. The contribution of the corporeal approach emerges from an ethics in organizations that is collective, other-focused, and generous. This ethics is fundamentally based in embodied affect, yet practically materialized in ethico-political acts of positive resistance and revitalization.

References

Acker, J. (1990) Hierarchies, jobs, bodies: A theory of gendered organizations. *Gender & Society*, 4(2): 139–158.

Acker, J. (2006). Inequality regimes: Gender, class, and race in organizations. *Gender & Society*, 20(4): 441–464.

Barker, R.A. (2002) An examination of organizational ethics. *Human Relations*, 55(9): 1097–1116.

Barnett, C., and Land, D. (2007) Geographies of generosity: Beyond the 'moral turn'. *Geoforum*, 38(6): 1065–1075.

Beasley, C., and Bacchi, C. (2007) Envisaging a new politics for an ethical future: Beyond trust, care and generosity—towards an ethic of social flesh. *Feminist Theory*, 8(3): 279–298.

Bell, E., Taylor, S., and Driscoll, C. (2012) Varieties of organizational soul: The ethics of belief in organizations. *Organization*, 19(4): 425–439.

Bigo, V. (2018) On silence, creativity and ethics in organization studies. *Organization Studies*, 39(1): 121–133.

Boling, T.E. (1978) The management ethics 'crisis': An organizational perspective. *Academy of Management Review*, 3(2): 360–365.

Britton, D.M., and Logan, L. (2008) Gendered organizations: Progress and prospects. *Sociology Compass*, 2(1): 107–121.

Butler, J. (2015) *Notes Toward a Performative Theory of Assembly*. Cambridge: Harvard University Press.

Carlson, D.S., and Perrewe, P.L. (1995) Institutionalization of organizational ethics through transformational leadership. *Journal of Business Ethics*, 14(10): 829–938.

Clegg, S.R., Kornberger, M., and Rhodes, C. (2007) Business ethics as practice. *British Journal of Management*, 18: 107–122.

Constantinescu, M., and Kaptein, M. (2020) Ethics management and ethical management: Mapping criteria and interventions to support responsible management practice. In O. Laasch, R. Suddaby, R.E. Freeman, and D. Jamali (Eds.), pp. 155–174, *Research Handbook of Responsible Management*. Cheltenham: Edward Elgar.

De Coster, M. (2020) Towards a relational ethics in pandemic times and beyond: Limited accountability, collective performativity and new subjectivity. *Gender, Work and Organization*, 27(5): 747–753.

Diprose, M. (2002) *Corporeal Generosity: On Giving with Nietzsche, Merleau-Ponty and Levinas*. Albany, NY: State University of New York Press.

Diprose, R. (1994) *The Bodies of Women: Ethics, Embodiment and Sexual Differences*. London: Routledge.

Diprose, R. (2013) Corporeal interdependence: From vulnerability to dwelling in ethical community. *SubStance*, 42(3): 185–204.

Dunne, S., Harney, S., and Parker, M. (2008) Speaking out: The responsibilities of management intellectuals: A survey, *Organization*, 15(2): 271–282.

Fatien Diochon, P., Defiebre-Muller, R., and Viola, F. (2018) Toward an 'ethics of serendipity': Disrupting normative ethical discourses in organizations. *Human Resource Development Review*, 17(4): 373–392.

Fleming, P., and Spicer, A. (2003) Working at a cynical distance: Implications for power, surveillance and resistance. *Organization*, 10: 157–179.

Fotaki, M., Metcalfe, B.D., and Harding, N. (2014) Writing materiality into management and organization studies through and with Luce Irigaray. *Human Relations*, 67(10): 1239–1263.

Gatens, K. (1996) *Imaginary Bodies: Ethics, Power, and Corporeality*. New York: Routledge.

Gordon, R., Clegg, S., and Kornberger, M. (2009) Embedded ethics: Discourse and power in the New South Wales Police Service. *Organization Studies*, 30(1): 73–99.

Grosz, E. (1994) *Volatile Bodies: Toward a Corporeal Feminism*. Indianapolis: Indiana University Press.

Hancock, P. (2008) Embodied generosity and an ethics of organization. *Organization Studies*, 29(10): 1357–1373.

Hartman, E.M. (2001) Moral philosophy, political philosophy, and organizational ethics: A response to Phillips and Margolis. *Business Ethics Quarterly*, 11(4): 673–685.

Heath, E., Kaldis, B., and Marcoux, A. (Eds.) (2018) *The Routledge Companion to Business Ethics*. London: Routledge.

Helin, S., and Sandstrom, J. (2010) Resisting a corporate code of ethics and the reinforcement of management control. *Organization Studies*, 31(5): 583–604.

Iedema, R., and Rhodes, C. (2010) The undecided space of ethics in organizational surveillance. *Organization Studies*, 31(2): 199–217.

Jermier, J.M., Knights, D., and Nord, W.R. (Eds.) (1994) *Resistance and Power in Organizations*. London: Routledge.

Jones, C. (2003) As if business ethics were possible, 'within such limits' …. *Organization*, 10(2): 223–248.

Jose, A., and Thibodeaux, M.S. (1999) Institutionalization of ethics: The perspective of managers. *Journal of Business Ethics*, 22(2): 133–143.

Kenny, K., and Fotaki, M. (2015) From gendered organizations to compassionate borderspaces: Reading corporeal ethics with Bracha Ettinger. *Organization*, 22(2): 183–199.

Knights, D. (2015) Binaries need to shatter for bodies to matter: Do disembodied masculinities undermine organizational ethics? *Organization*, 22(2): 200–216.

Knights, D., and Pullen, A. (2019) Masculinity: A contested terrain? *Gender, Work & Organization*, 26(10): 1367–1375.

McCabe, D. (2019) The day of the rally: An ethnographic study of 'ceremony as resistance' and 'resistance as ceremony'. *Organization*, 26(2): 255–275.

McCarthy, E. (2010) *Ethics Embodied: Rethinking Selfhood through Continental, Japanese, and Feminist Philosophies*. Lexington Books.

McDaniel, C. (2001) *Organizational Ethics: Research and Ethical Environments*. Aldershot: Ashgate.

McLeod, M.S., Payne, G.T., and Evert, R.E. (2016) Organizational ethics research: A systematic review of methods and analytical techniques. *Journal of Business Ethics*, 134(3): 429–443.

McMurray, R., Pullen, A., and Rhodes, C. (2011) Ethical subjectivity and politics in organizations: A case of health care tendering. *Organization*, 18(4): 541–561.

Meriläinen, S., Tienari, J., Thomas, R., and Davies, A. (2004) Management consultant talk: A cross-cultural comparison of normalizing discourse and resistance, *Organization*, 11(4): 539–564.

Metzger, M., Dalton, D.R., and Hill, J.W. (1993) The organization of ethics and the ethics of organizations: The case for expanded organizational ethics audits. *Business Ethics Quarterly*, 3(1): 27–43.

Munro, I. (2014) Organizational ethics and Foucault's 'art of living': Lessons from social movement organizations. *Organization Studies*, 35(8): 1127–1148.

Nicotera, A.M., and Cushman, D.P. (1992) Organizational ethics: A within organization view. *Journal of Applied Communication Research*, 20(4): 437–462.

Nielsen, R.P. (2006) Introduction to the special issue. In search of organizational virtue: Moral agency in organizations. *Organization Studies*, 27(3): 317–321.

Phillips, M., Pullen, A., and Rhodes, C. (2014) Writing organization as gendered practice: Interrupting the libidinal economy. *Organization Studies*, 35(3): 313–333.

Phillips, R.A., and Margolis, J.D. (1999) Toward an ethics of organization. *Business Ethics Quarterly*, 9(4): 619–638.

Poldner, K., Branzei, O., and Steyaert, C. (2019) Fashioning ethical subjectivity: The embodied ethics of entrepreneurial self-formation. *Organization*, 26(2): 151–174.

Pullen, A. (2018) Writing as labiaplasty. *Organization*, 25(1): 123–130.

Pullen, A., and Rhodes, C. (Eds.) (2015a) *Routledge Companion to Ethics, Politics and Organization*. London: Routledge.

Pullen, A., and Rhodes, C. (2015b) Writing, the feminine and organization. *Gender, Work and Organization*, 22(2): 87–93.

Pullen, A., and Rhodes, C. (2015c) Ethics, embodiment and organization. *Organization*, 22(2): 159–165.

Pullen, A., Rhodes, C., and Thanem, T. (2017) Affective politics in gendered organizations: Affirmative notes on becoming-woman. *Organization*, 24(1): 105–123.

Rhodes, C. (2016) Democratic business ethics: Volkswagen's emissions scandal and the disruption of corporate sovereignty. *Organization Studies*, 37(10): 1501–1518.

Rhodes, C. (2019). *Disturbing Business Ethics: Emmanuel Levinas and the Politics of Organization*. Abingdon: Routledge.

Rhodes, C., Munro, I., Thanem, T., and Pullen, A. (2020) Dissensus! Radical democracy and business ethics. *Journal of Business Ethics*, 164: 627–632.

Rhodes, C., Pullen, A., and Clegg, S.R. (2010) 'If I should fall from grace …': Stories of change and organizational ethics. *Journal of Business Ethics*, 91(4): 535–551.

Roberts, J. (2001) Corporate governance and the ethics of narcissus. *Business Ethics Quarterly*, 11(1): 109–127.

Sharp, H. (2019) Feminism and heterodoxy: Moira Gatens's Spinoza. *Philosophy Today*, 63(3): 795–803.

Shildrick, M. (2015). *Leaky Bodies and Boundaries: Feminism, Postmodernism and (Bio) Ethics*. London: Routledge.

Sims, R.R. (1991) The institutionalization of organizational ethics. *Journal of Business Ethics*, 10(7): 493–506.

Smith, H.R., and Carroll, A.B. (1984) Organizational ethics: A stacked deck. *Journal of Business Ethics*, 3(2): 95–100.

Thanem, T., and Wallenberg, L. (2015) What can bodies do? Reading Spinoza for an affective ethics of organizational life. *Organization*, 22(2): 235–250.

Thomas, R., and Linstead, A. (2002) Losing the plot? Middle managers and identity. *Organization*, 9(1): 71–93.

Tyler, M. (2019) *Judith Butler and Organization Theory*. London: Routledge.

Vachhani, S.J., and Pullen, A. (2019) Ethics, politics and feminist organizing: Writing feminist infrapolitics and affective solidarity into everyday sexism. *Human Relations*, 72(1): 23–47.

Verkerk, M.J., De Leede, J., and Nijhof, A.H.J. (2001) From responsible management to responsible organizations: The democratic principle for managing organizational ethics. *Business and Society Review*, 106(4): 353–378.

Vitell, S.J., and Singhapakdi, A. (2008) The role of ethics institutionalization in influencing organizational commitment, job satisfaction, and Esprit de Corps. *Journal of Business Ethics*, 81(2): 343–353.

Weber, J. (1993) Institutionalizing ethics into business organizations: A model and research agenda. *Business Ethics Quarterly*, 3(4): 419–436.

Weiskopf, R., and Willmott, H. (2013) Ethics as critical practice: The 'Pentagon Papers', deciding responsibly, truth-telling, and the unsettling of organizational morality. *Organization Studies*, 34(4): 469–493.

Wempe, B. (2008) Contractarian business ethics: Credentials and design criteria. *Organization Studies*, 29(10): 1337–1355.

Westwood, R., and Johnston, A. (2012) Reclaiming authentic selves: Control, resistive humour and identity work in the office. *Organization Studies*, 9(6): 787–808.

Wicks, A.C., and Freeman, R.E. (1998) Organization studies and the new pragmatism: Positivism, antipositivism and the search for ethics. *Organization Science*, 9(2): 123–140.

Wray-Bliss, E. (2009) Ethics: Critique, ambivalence and infinite responsibilities (unmet). In M. Alvesson, T. Bridgman, and H. Willmott (Eds.), pp. 267–285, *The Oxford Handbook of Critical Management Studies*. Oxford: Oxford University Press.

2   Corporeal ethics and organizations

To consider ethics as corporeal attests to the idea that the original impulse that moves us to act for the benefit of others without prior or primary consideration of ourselves arises as an affective and embodied feeling. The desire for such action is not a result of rational calculation, moral deliberation, or ethical reasoning. It is a more fundamental and affirmative response to the needs of other people. Corporeal ethics begins pre-reflectively and before one's own ego. This ethics can manifest in productive actions such as caring for, protecting, and helping others. I can also inform actions that preserve one's own well-being and ability to act for others, for example, walking away from destructive relationships, or disengaging people whose actions result in hurt or harm.

This starting point is very different from the more established conceptions of what constitutes ethics. Rosalyn Diprose explains:

> Ethics, as a branch of Anglophone philosophy, has tended to focus on the nature of moral judgement (to secure its rational basis) or on the nature of the moral principles which do or should govern social relations (to secure their universal status). Behind this inquiry lies the conviction that a moral code can and should maintain our social order, protecting it against transgression and disintegration.
>
> (Diprose, 1994: v)

Chapter 1 discussed the history of the ethics of organizations, albeit much more recent than ethics per se, has developed in line with this philosophical tradition. Advocates for organizational ethics have steadfastly proclaimed the value of establishing ethical decision-making processes (see O'Fallon and Butterfield, 2005; Ferrell et al., 2014) and codes and frameworks for ethical behaviour (cf. Roberts, 2003). The

DOI: 10.4324/9781003031048-2

main form of reasoning is that if organizations and their members were to follow the right processes and precepts, ethicality could be ensured and responsibility achieved. Moreover, such renderings of ethics and responsibility have become institutionalized expectations in organizations; they simply cannot be avoided by the socially valid corporations (Brammer et al., 2012), many of who take public pride in asserting just how good they really think they are (Fleming et al., 2013).

A turn to corporeal ethics questions this ethics in a fundamental way, proposing that the reduction of ethics to being only instantiated through rational judgement and codification too often results in oppressive practices and are blind to injustices that do not affect or concern the powerful (Diprose, 1994). That is not to say there should be no place for ethical rules and norms in organizations. Indeed, it is through such practices that fair and equal outcomes can be pursued, especially as it relates to the possibility of organization justice (cf. Rhodes, 2012). Despite this, it is a mistake to assert that ethics of organization should somehow apply to all people in all places without the embodied lives and experiences of those people being accounted for. It is also a mistake to suggest that this form of ethics exhausts the possibility for ethical action. The hubris that would pretend that a complete ethics could be determined in an entirely a priori and speculative fashion is no part of corporeal ethics. Indeed, 'it is an unavoidable (and welcome) consequence of constructing an embodied ethics that ethics would no longer pretend to be universal' (Gatens, 1996: 56).

Irrespective of whether theorists of organizational ethics might posit or imply such universal ethics, it is to the actual practices of and within organizations that corporeal ethics responds. Notably, organizational practices that are nominally related to ethics and justice have been shown, in many instances, to be very questionable ethically. At worst ethics is rendered as a tool of managerial control it can be used to 'legitimate the power of large corporations' and 'regulate the behaviour of stakeholders' (Banerjee, 2008: 52–53). Further, when organizations seek to define the interests of others in their own terms so that they can be controlled for the benefit of the corporation itself, then an ethics of genuine concern and respect for other people lies in tatters. In place, we have what has been called a 'market for virtue' such that ethics is engaged in because it makes business sense to do so (Vogel, 2008), a matter explored in more depth in Chapter 3. For now, it is sufficient to say that even though ethics and responsibility might be all the rage among global corporate elites, this is concurrent with and supportive of an era of rampant corporate power, greed, violence, scandal, and mistrust.

With this chapter, we sketch the contours of corporeal ethics as it is relevant to organizations. This corporeal approach, as it has increasingly been taken up in organizations studies (e.g. Dale and Latham, 2015; Kenny and Fotaki, 2015; Poldner et al., 2019; Tyler, 2019), forms a political corrective to the expanding limits of managerial ethical and political prerogative. To pursue this, we first examine organizational ethics as it has, in line with the dominant Western philosophical tradition, been associated with rationality and judgement. We also consider how such ethics, when used in organizations, can serve as a means through which organizations deploy ethics to pursue self-interest. Corporeal ethics is put forward as both an antidote and a supplement to this self-interested ethics, drawing especially from recent scholarship in organization studies on corporeal and embodied ethics. To make sense of this accounts of embodied and corporeal ethics in contemporary feminist philosophy are reviewed, most especially those related to 'corporeal feminism' (Grosz, 1994; Gatens, 1996; Diprose, 2002) establish the connection between corporeal ethics and political activity in organizations. On that basis, we suggest that the practical import of corporeal ethics in organizations concerns an ethico-political resistance to the forms of oppression, discrimination, and injustice based on a closing down of difference.

Ethics before authority and self-interest

Criticisms that practices of ethics and responsibility in organizations can be rationalized and self-serving are well established (Rhodes, 2016). In the previous chapter, we discussed that ethics of organizations is commonly premised on the idea that organizations can and should plan and implement ethical programmes that would sure up corporate morality. As we also saw, with such an approach ethical agency rests exclusively with executive authority, with those subject to that authority expected to conform. The result is that political contestation or deliberation over what constitutes ethicality is downplayed, especially as it might be enacted outside of centres of power. The result is that ethics becomes associated with consensus and conformity (Rhodes and Wray-Bliss, 2013).

Organizational ethics, as it is practised, has also come under criticism for being self-interested; at worst a means through which organizations can extend their power by using self-regulation as a means of minimizing legal and regulatory control (Hanlon and Fleming, 2009: 937). Ethics thus becomes yoked to authority when organizations both implement and proclaim ethical practice to bolster their own sovereignty

(Rhodes, 2016). In such cases, ethics is used for self-advantage, either exclusively, or through a less direct approach that requires a business case to be established prior to any nominally ethical programme being undertaken. In response, it has been argued that if organizational ethics involves the calculation of organizational advantage that results from ethical acts, then the possibility for organizational ethics is strictly limited (Jones, 2003; Rhodes and Westwood, 2016).

Such forms of self-interested ethics have criticized on account of their narcissism (Roberts, 2003) and their primary focus on enhancing corporate legitimacy and power (Shamir, 2008). There is also a recognized concern that the focus on a self-interested organizational ethics is limited precisely because of its privileging of reason over emotion (ten Bos and Willmott, 2001), rules over relationships (Loacker and Muhr, 2009), a priori judgement over contextualized experience (Borgerson, 2007), and the mind over the body (Bevan and Corvellec, 2007; Hancock, 2008). An approach to ethics that privileges reciprocal self-interest, planning, predictability, control, and measurement seems to forget the value of affectual relations, care, compassion, or any other forms of feeling that are experienced pre-reflexively through the body (Pullen and Rhodes, 2010; Pullen et al., 2017). Instead, ethics is reduced to a matter of impersonal dealings within a masculine 'economy of contract and exchange' (Diprose, 2002: 6), where corporations act on behalf of their putative selves, only willing to give when they can calculate a greater return.

The critique of the rationalization of ethics, such as that which has taken place in the organization studies literature, emerges from the idea that a universal, rational or codifiable model for ethics is a result of thinking is both masculine and disembodied (cf. Diprose, 2002). The point is that ethics can be approached through an ongoing questioning of 'conventional notions of moral agency, autonomy, justice, and freedom and the concept of the individual upon which they depend: the self who governs and owns property in their body' (Diprose, 1994: ix). A similar questioning is relevant to organizations, those institutions that have always been dominated by men and masculinity both materially and symbolically (Acker, 1990; Pullen et al., 2017). Shouldn't we expect that if organizations are culturally masculine that their ethics would also be masculine, in the sense of being dominated by desires for control, rationality and order? This would be an ethics developed by and for the 'man of reason' who privileges the mind over the body and equates masculinity with universality (Lloyd, 1993).

The critique of a rational-masculine ethics of control and the re-thinking of ethics from an embodied perspective as it has occurred in feminist theory and philosophy (e.g. Diprose, 1994; Gatens, 1996; Shildrick, 1997; Hamington, 2004) has deeply informed our own perspective on organizational ethics. This stimulates an interest in what might happen when an ethics founded in and through the human body encounters the rationalized and routinized character of organizations (Pullen and Rhodes, 2010). In the wake of what was been dubbed an 'ethical turn' in social theory (Garber et al., 2000), the corporeal character of ethics as manifest in an 'ethico-political' practice becomes our focus (Diprose, 2002; Parker, 2003; Pullen et al., 2017). Calling into question the controlling and rational nature of traditional ethical theorizing as an 'ethics that is out of touch with the body' (Shildrick, 1997: 172), the corporeal ethics advanced is one that arises from the interaction between people (with all the diversity involved), the embodied effects and affects of that interaction and the indissoluble relation between thinking and feeling.

Two decades ago Roberts (2001) argued that the dominant practice of organizational ethics was one that seeks the appearance of ethics without grappling with the lived, sensed, and felt experience of inter-personal ethical engagement. This rationalized and instrumental approach, Roberts evinced, failed to recognize that 'within and beyond the imaginary surface of the corporate body, lie sensible and vulnerable bodies' (p. 125). Moreover, it is through such sensibility that we can begin to extend our understanding of how ethics might play out in organizations. Roberts concluded that the ethical challenge was 'to break the mirror in which we mistakenly conceive of interests as internal to the self or corporation, and allow us to make use of the real corporeal sensibility that knows interests to be always inter-esse' (p. 125); that is to be 'in between' and relational.

Since Roberts alerted us to the disembodied and individualistic character of organizational ethics, there has been much work to remedy this, as well as to go against the grain of more rationalist and instrumental approaches. In organization studies, the parallel growth of interest in studying the body (see Gärtner, 2013) and ethics (see Rhodes and Wray-Bliss, 2013) has begun to cross with attention to the corporeal nature of ethics having been increasingly attended to directly. The opportunity this has opened is for a 'reversal of the traditional principle on which Morality [that] was founded as an enterprise of domination of the passions by consciousness' (Deleuze, 1988: 18) to be brought to bear on the study of organizations through connecting the body with ethics.

Within the organization studies literature, studies of corporeal ethics have variously addressed topics such as gender and organization

(Kenny and Fotaki, 2015; Knights, 2015), difference and inclusion (Tyler, 2019), women's embodied labour (Lee, 2018), and entrepreneurial subjectivity (Poldner et al., 2019). These projects share a political sensibility that engages with the material effects of embodied and affective experience at work. This sensibility enables a more engaged, compassionate, resistant, and pluralistic ethics that counters strong organizational tendencies towards control, homogeneity, discrimination, and domination. Importantly, corporeal ethics does not propose a universal solution, and neither does it submit to a desire for one. In place of these tendencies lies the possibilities for an ethics which is embodied, social, relational, and embedded in its local contexts and situational particularities – what we call corporeal ethics. Moreover, this concern with an ethics of the body is one that engages with materiality, the fleshy substance of the human body as well as its relation to the material of the world and of non-human bodies, such as our relations with our dogs Ted and Rupert (see Levinas, 1990/1975 for an especially moving account of relations between humans and animals).

As an example, a study by Karen Dale and Yvonne Latham (2015) developed corporeal ethics in relation to research in an organization that supports the social integration of people with disabilities. They draw special attention to embodiment as it relates to race, sex, physical ability, and age, as well as how forms of difference that are outside of the organizational norm become common sources of oppression and discrimination. The corporeal ethics that Dale and Latham identify in this context is rooted in a responsibility to overcome inequalities written on the body by organizations themselves. The uptake of this ethics is political, Dale and Latham argue, in that it serves to contest and disturb organizations in actual encounters between people and their (different) bodies. Such a politics is, however, always grounded in ethics and responsibility to others that take form in 'concrete relations made of care, compassion, generosity, and any forms of feeling experienced pre-reflexively through the body' so as to resist domination and the pursuit of self-interest at others' expense (Faldetta, 2018).

Drawing on the work of Judith Butler, Melissa Tyler (2019) specifically addresses corporeal ethics as it relates to diversity and inclusion in organizations. Tyler draws attention to how inclusion can be read as a 'normative regime' that members of organizations are compelled to conform with in order that diversity and difference can be incorporated organizationally. Difference is thus codified and managed, with some forms of difference recognized and others marginalized. Tyler's position is that 'the basis of our ethical relationship to one another is our embodied interconnection and the mutual, corporeal vulnerability that arises from this' (p. 51). This relational conception of ethics jars with approaches to inclusion premised on the codification of difference, and the attendant power relations they produce. Inclusion, by Tyler's account, needs to be ethically reimagined to move beyond its organizational regulation and towards a more embodied relational practice.

Care needs to be taken not to imagine that corporeal ethics in organization is something that occurs only in individual interactions, but can also be collective in spirit (Pérezts et al., 2015). Sheena Vachhani and Alison Pullen (2019) make clear, corporeal ethics is very much a matter of embodied solidarity as well. As they aver with specific reference to ethical resistance to sexism in organizations: 'ethico-politics of feminist resistance moves away from individualizing experiences of sexism towards collective resistance and organizes solidarity, experience and empathy that may combat ignorance and violence towards women' (p. 23). It is through such solidarity that embodied compassion and care for others develop into a social sensibility that provides a means to mobilize 'solidarity based on affective, embodied experiences in the resistance against sexism' (p. 26).

Collectively, these examples demonstrate that a corporeal ethics of organization is also an ethics of difference; specifically one that recognizes compassion, connectedness, and care as the ethical basis on which to oppose structures and practices of normalization and domination of people rendered 'other' (Kenny and Fotaki, 2015). This ethics is a necessary tension with modes of organizing that have been traditionally masculine, not only in that they have been dominated by men, but also because they have privileged the mind over the body, the objective over the subjective, and the rational over the emotional (cf. Acker, 1990). It is in dissolving these differences on ethical grounds that domination can be overcome by opening the self to difference through engaged and embodied relations at work (Knights, 2015). The trajectory that this embarks on is directed at enhancing individual and collective joy and power (Thanem and Wallenberg, 2015).

Corporeal ethics

To provide more detailed theoretical ground on which to imagine a corporeal ethics of organization we now turn in more depth to theorizations of the relations between the body and ethics as they can be found in feminist philosophy, most especially as it is associated with what has been termed 'Australian corporeal feminism' (Colebrook, 2000; MacCormack, 2009). This feminism, as has been developed in the work of philosophers such as Moira Gatens, Elizabeth Grosz, Genevieve Lloyd, and Rosalyn Diprose, can be defined through 'an inextricable encounter between flesh and psyche, the social body and the bodily polis' (MacCormack, 2009: 86). Corporeal feminism is explicitly political in that it:

> emphasizes the ontological aspect of difference feminism by participating in the continental critique of the opposition between idealism and realism to reveal how gender discrimination operates, not by force or by corrupting the minds of citizens with spurious ideas of gender, but via the 'institution' of the sexed body.
>
> (Diprose, 2012: 227)

The implications are beyond gender discrimination, with a central theme within this having been a reconsideration of the meaning of ethics as it relates primarily to the relations between embodied people in material and social contexts. This deliberately counters the way that, traditionally, ethics has been 'marred by its indifference to the specificities of gender, race, class, sexuality and so on' (Shildrick, 1997: 63).

Claire Colebrook offers a clear explanation of the place of the body in the ethics of corporeal feminism:

> Within the corporeal feminist tradition, the body, as both material and sexed, is inextricable from ethics insofar as ethics is understood as the tangled relatedness of humanity, and the capacity of our embodied interactions to be driven by a care for other people. Central is the idea that ethics is always a matter of situated action and interaction that does not rest on the false laurels of an assumed universal set of ethical precepts, rules or virtues that might guide people's morality irrespective of who or where they are. This leaves us with: an understanding of ethics, not as the telos of some universal law, but as the responsibility and recognition of the self-formation of the body. This self-formation does not take the form of a transparent will thoroughly determining itself [...] the becoming of the human is sexually embodied, historically located, and politically related.
>
> (Colebrook, 2000: 88)

Moira Gatens (1996) explains further that the bodies of women and children have traditionally been denied ethical and political status within the 'body politic' such that the assumed neutrality and universality of ethics mask its masculinity. The cultural distinction that remains is the 'division between the (bodily, natural, feminine) private sphere and the (rational, cultural, masculine) public sphere' (p. 57). Organizations and their ethics are placed firmly in the latter category as we have contended earlier. Gatens counters this division by declaring ethics as being directly concerned with embodiment in a manner that is prior to the 'political organization of ethics and prior to the conceptualization of ethics as reducible to a set of universal principles dictated by reason (whose reason?)' (p. 26). That which is prior is an ethics based on a concern for other people – not in general, but real flesh and blood people whose lives intersect with ours. For Gatens this concern for others is the 'primitive core' of ethics.

The fundamental question of ethics, as Elizabeth Grosz (in Grosz and Hill, 2017) explains, concerns 'our manner of living in the world with others' (p. 8) in a way that is tied to our very existence as it is 'dependent on a great chain of others on whom one's existence depends and which one's existence affects' (p. 11). Such an ethics is emergent from one's place in the world and one's relationships with other people. It is corporeal in the sense that it:

> enables humans to not only to make the most of their corporeal abilities – to grow, sustain themselves, reproduce, act, make – but also to make the most of that body within us that is the soul or psyche, which is capable, through language, of apprehending the ordered nature of the world, its possibilities, and the inevitability of it changing.
>
> (Grosz, 2017: 52)

The ethics that is developed in corporeal feminism is one that is located in the interaction of bodies, and their differences. It is also an ethics that denies the desire for universalism, instead placing ethics in real encounters between different people in actual situations. Because of this, corporeal ethics will 'inevitably accommodate the production of embodied specificity in all of its political and ethical configurations' (Hinton, 2013: 184), including in our case, organizational configurations.

Rosalyn Diprose, in her book *Corporeal Generosity* (2002), explicitly develops an approach to ethics grounded in embodied lived experience, as well as one that is especially relevant to considering an ethics of organization. This is an ethics that is 'at the foundation of social existence' (p. 14) rather than one that comes from social organization and its deliberate management. Diprose's ideas are a central influence on our conception of a corporeal ethics of organization. In so doing we

acknowledge that studies of corporeal ethics in the organizations studies literature have drawn on a broad variety of theoretical influences,
including the work of Emmanuel Levinas (Faldetta, 2018), Judith Butler (Tyler, 2019), Maurice Merleau-Ponty (Hancock, 2008), Bracha Ettinger (Kenny and Fotaki, 2015), and Baruch Spinoza (Thanem and
Wallenberg, 2015). Within corporeal feminism there is also a diversity
of theoretical influences and ethical positions that overlap with these.

Diprose's work, in particular, shaped our thinking because of how
its explicit politics of radical difference is of direct relevance to the
issue of organizational ethics that we have been discussing so far. This
is so because Diprose's politics works towards dispelling forms of violent categorization and hierarchization that privilege those few who
are able to conform to the power of that which is institutionalized as
normal. This ethically informed politics invites us to work against the
conventions of culture that establish 'privileged ways of being, including one's own, thereby reducing sexed or cultural identity to isolate,
corporeal units, singled out for exchange, usury, judgement, correc-
tion, condemnation or ridicule' (2002: 194). Most especially Diprose
(2012) provides the grounds for 'thinking the corporeal with the political' by working towards a deinstitutionalization of the structures of
bodily difference that underpin inequality and discrimination, as well
as understanding generosity as an openness to others that exceeds the
cost-benefit analysis of reciprocal giving (Hird, 2010).

Diprose considers the body as the primary site of perception as 'per-
ceptual faith is guaranteed by the flesh' (2006: 36). Here Diprose is
referring to the sensate body; a body both in and of the world, and that
experiences and lives in that world. The body, and its interaction with
and dependence on other bodies, makes for the 'system of intercorporeality' (2002: 90) where ethics begins. This pre-reflective embodied
interaction is one where to be ethical is to embrace a desire to respond
to the other with generosity before thinking about one's own advantage and before imposing organizational schemes (see also Faldetta,
2018). Such giving is not a matter of a sovereign subject donating his
or her possessions to others. Generosity, in Diprose's (2002) account
of it, is not about giving over a 'calculable commodity' (p. 2) but is
'an openness to others that not only precedes and establishes communal relations but constitutes the self as open to otherness' (p. 4). This
generosity is corporeal to the extent that it is pre-reflective, affective,
and embodied, and is ethical to the extent that it is an 'other-directed
sensibility' (p. 14) that is not only virtuous but also a condition of
human existence. To be clear, considering ethics 'as a prereflective
corporeal openness to otherness' (p. 5) does not mean that it is just
some sort of reflex physical reaction, but rather that it originates in an

embodied relationship with other people that, in turn, constitutes who we are individually and communally.

Following Diprose, ethics comes to bear on the intercorporeal relations between people and prior to their categorization, normalization, and regulation as subjects, as it might be achieved, for example, through a normalizing organization of ethics. Such normalizing would be tantamount to 'moralizing that fails its body by finishing itself through vampirism of other' (Diprose, 2002: 195). This vampirism meaning that the other is consumed into one's own systems of (ethical) knowledge rather than being welcomed in an always-emerging set of relations. Diprose's corporeal generosity arises by encountering and responding to the 'other'. Otherness refers to particular embodied others to whom we relate in social interactions; not a generalized other representing the community but a concrete other; an actual other person (cf. Benhabib, 1992). Ethical primacy is given to the embodied other in self-other relations as opposed to obscuring particular individual relationships through generalization and the organization of people into comparable categories.

Diprose's generosity is taken up by 'promoting ways to foster social relations that generate rather than close off sexual, cultural, and stylistic differences' (2002: 15). This begs the question of how organizational relations might rely on openness to difference based on a 'welcoming of the alterity of the ethical relation' (Diprose, 2002: 140), potentially in spite of those managerial and ethical programmes that are deployed at an organizational level. These relations arise not in a 'meeting of minds' but from intercorporeal encounters that problematize the relationship between self/other and identity/body. Ethically, this becomes 'a means of redressing social discrimination and normalization' (p. 11); the normalization that takes the form of institutionalization that many business and organizational ethicists have actually advocated as the means to ethicality. Our attention becomes drawn towards a politics based on corporeal generosity that is not so much about such forms of institutionalization as it is about disrupting the taken-for-granted means through which moral judgement is imposed. Disruption marks the ethico-politics of resistance to normalization as well as a resistance to the social inequalities that these (re)produce.

From ethics to politics

The corporeality of generosity that informs Diprose's ethico-politics stems from an understanding of bodily practice that precedes rationality and intellect (and hence precedes also organization) in an affective dimension where bodies move and respond to other bodies while recognizing them as unassimilable. Generosity does not proceed from a calculation of one's own advantage in giving; if it was it would negate itself as true generosity and become only a mode of exchange (see Rhodes and Westwood, 2016). With corporeal ethics, it is not the management and organization of ethics that is privileged; the focus is on the politically engaged affective body that responds openly and positively to others without always considering the self first.

Diprose accounts for how the meaning of an ethics of hospitality and generosity might inform everyday life. Exploring 'ethico-politics' as that arena where ethics is mobilized into action creates a politics directed by ethics. Diprose's ethico-politics is concerned with forms of resistance and critique of 'familiar ideas'; that is those ideas that close down an openness to alterity by constraining the unknowability of the other with rigid categories and preconceived notions. For Diprose, corporeal ethics enacts a generosity that is an overflowing 'life force' which resists and 'defies the culturally informed habits of perception and judgement that would perpetuate injustice by shoring up body integrity, singular identity, and their distinction between inside and outside, culture and nature, self and other' (Diprose, 2002: 190). This is an ethically grounded resistance to forms of moral discipline and regulation that seek to bring people into line with pre-designed norms and values. In some cases, this would include the masculine norms and values discussed earlier in relation to designs for an ethics of organization.

Instead of telling people what they ought to do or who they ought to be so as to be judged as ethical, corporeal generosity disrupts the self because it is a 'prereflective activity mediated by the cultural-historical that haunts my perception, but an activity that surpasses that perception and the modes of being that it supports' (Diprose, 2002: 193). For Diprose ethico-politics involves resisting the shoring up of norms and values that coagulate the self-rendering it unable to openly welcome the other in generosity. Doing so 'provides a way of restoring to human elements of "life," not control over life, but the burden of responsibility for keeping the world open for ethics' (Diprose, 2009: 8). It is this restorative resistance that marks the practical uptake of corporeal ethics such that it can combat the forms of oppression and discrimination that result from closing down difference, especially at the hands of power and authority. Moreover, it is the exercise of such an ethico-politics that can bring corporeal ethics to life in organizations, rendering them a plural and democratically vital site through which respect and care for others can be enacted.

References

Acker, J. (1990) Hierarchies, jobs, bodies: A theory of gendered organizations. *Gender and Society*, 4(2): 139–158.

Banerjee, S.B. (2008) Corporate social responsibility: The good, the bad and the ugly. *Critical Sociology*, 34(1): 51–79.

Benhabib, S. (1992) *Situating the Self: Gender, Community and Postmodernism in Contemporary Ethics*. Cambridge: Polity.

Bevan, D., and Corvellec, H. (2007) The impossibility of corporate ethics: For a Levinasian approach to managerial ethics. *Business Ethics: A European Review*, 16(3): 208–219.

Borgerson, J.L. (2007) On the harmony of feminist ethics and business ethics. *Business and Society* Review, 112(4): 477–509.

Brammer, S., Jackson, G., and Matten, D. (2012) Corporate social responsibility and institutional theory: New perspectives on private governance. *Socio-Economic Review*, 10(1): 3–28.

Colebrook, C. (2000). From radical representations to corporeal becomings: The feminist philosophy of Lloyd, Grosz, and Gatens. *Hypatia*, 15(2): 76–93.

Dale, K., and Latham, Y. (2015) Ethics and entangled embodiment: Bodies–materialities–organization. *Organization*, 22(2): 166–182.

Deleuze, G. (1988) *Spinoza: Practical Philosophy* (trans. R. Hurley). San Francisco, CA: City Light Books.

Diprose, R. (1994) *The Bodies of Women: Ethics, Embodiment and Sexual Difference*. London: Routledge.

Diprose, R. (2002) *Corporeal Generosity: On Giving With Nietzsche, Merleau-Ponty and Levinas*. New York: State University of New York Press.

Diprose, R. (2006) The art of dreaming: Merleau-Ponty and Petyarre on flesh expressing a world. *Cultural Studies Review*, 12(1): 32–43.

Diprose, R. (2009) Toward an ethico-politics of the posthuman: Foucault and Merleau-Ponty. *Parrhesia*, 8: 7–19.

Diprose, R. (2012) Continental philosophy: Thinking the corporeal with the political. *The Southern Journal of Philosophy*, 50(2): 220–233.

Faldetta, G. (2018) A relational approach to responsibility in organizations: The logic of gift and Levinasian ethics for a 'corporeal' responsibility. *Culture and Organization*, 24(3): 196–220.

Ferrell, O.C., Fraedrich, J., and Ferrell, L. (2014) *Business Ethics: Ethical Decision Making and Cases*. Stamford, CT: Cengage Learning.

Fleming, P., Roberts, J., and Garsten, C. (2013) In search of corporate social responsibility. *Organization*, 20(3): 337–348.

Garber, M., Hanssen, B., and Walkowitz, W.L. (2000) *The Turn to Ethics*. New York: Routledge.

Gärtner, C. (2013) Cognition, knowing and learning in the flesh: Six views on embodied knowing in organization studies. *Scandinavian Journal of Management*, 29(4): 338–352.

Gatens, M. (1996) *Imaginary Bodies: Ethics, Power and Corporeality*. Abington, MA: Routledge.

Grosz, E. (1994) *Volatile Bodies: Toward A Corporeal Feminism.* St Leonards, NSW: Allen and Unwin.

Grosz, E. (2017) *The Incorporeal: Ontology, Ethics, and the Limits of Materialism.* New York: Columbia University Press.

Grosz, E., and Hill, R. (2017) Onto-ethics and difference: An interview with Elizabeth Grosz. *Australian Feminist Law Journal,* 43(1): 5–14.

Hamington, M. (2004) *Embodied Care: Jane Addams, Maurice Merleau-Ponty, and Feminist Ethics.* Champaign: University of Illinois Press.

Hancock, P. (2008) Embodied generosity and an ethics of organization. *Organization Studies,* 29(10): 1357–1373.

Hanlon, G., and Fleming, P. (2009) Updating the critical perspective on corporate social responsibility. *Sociology Compass,* 3(6): 937–948.

Hinton, P. (2013) The quantum dance and the world's 'extraordinary liveliness': Refiguring corporeal ethics in Karen Barad's agential realism. *Somatechnics,* 3(1): 169–189.

Hird, M.J. (2010) The life of the gift. *Parallax,* 16(1): 1–6.

Jones, C. (2003) As if business ethics were possible, 'within such limits'. *Organization,* 10(2): 223–248.

Kenny, K., and Fotaki, M. (2015) From gendered organizations to compassionate borderspaces: Reading corporeal ethics with Bracha Ettinger. *Organization,* 22(2): 183–199.

Knights, D. (2015) Binaries need to shatter for bodies to matter: Do disembodied masculinities undermine organizational ethics? *Organization,* 22(2): 200–216.

Lee, R. (2018). Breastfeeding bodies: intimacies at work. *Gender, Work & Organization,* 25(1): 77–90.

Levinas, E. (1990/1975) The name of a dog, or natural rights. In E. Levinas (Ed.), pp. 151–153, *Difficult Freedom: Essays on Judaism.* Baltimore, MD: The Johns Hopkins University Press.

Lloyd, G. (1993) *The Man of Reason: 'Male' and 'Female' in Western Philosophy.* Minneapolis: University of Minnesota Press.

Loacker, B., and Muhr, S.L. (2009) How can I become a responsible subject? Towards a practice-based ethics of responsiveness. *Journal of Business Ethics,* 90(2): 265–277.

MacCormack, P. (2009) Feminist becomings: Hybrid feminism and haecceitic (re)production. *Australian Feminist Studies,* 24(59): 85–97.

O'Fallon, M.J., and Butterfield, K.D. (2005) A review of the empirical ethical decision-making literature: 1996–2003. *Journal of Business Ethics,* 59(4): 375–413.

Parker, M. (2003) Introduction: Ethics, politics and organizing. *Organization,* 10(2): 187–203.

Pérezts, M., Faÿ, E., and Picard, S. (2015) Ethics, embodied life and esprit de corps: An ethnographic study with anti-money laundering analysts. *Organization,* 22(2): 217–234.

Poldner, K., Branzei, O., and Steyaert, C. (2019). Fashioning ethical subjectivity: The embodied ethics of entrepreneurial self-formation. *Organization,* 26(2): 151–174.

Pullen, A., and Rhodes, C. (2010) Gender, mask and the face. In P. Lewis and R. Simpson (Eds.), pp. 233–248, *Revealing and Concealing Gender: Issues of Visibility in Organizations*. Basingstoke: Palgrave.

Pullen, A. and Rhodes, C. (Eds.) (2015) *The Routledge Companion to Ethics, Politics and Organization*. London: Routledge.

Pullen, A., Rhodes, C., and Thanem, T. (2017) Affective politics in gendered organizations: Affirmative notes on becoming-woman. *Organization*, 24(1): 105–123.

Rhodes, C. (2012) Ethics, alterity and the rationality of leadership justice. *Human Relations*, 65(10): 1311–1331.

Rhodes, C. (2016) Democratic business ethics: Volkswagen's emissions scandal and the disruption of corporate sovereignty. *Organization Studies*, 37(10): 1501–1518.

Rhodes, C., and Westwood, R. (2016). The limits of generosity: Lessons on ethics, economy, and reciprocity in Kafka's the metamorphosis. *Journal of Business Ethics*, 133(2): 235–248.

Rhodes, C., and Wray-Bliss, E. (2013) The ethical difference of organization. *Organization*, 20(1): 39–50.

Roberts, J. (2001) Corporate governance and the ethics of narcissus. *Business Ethics Quarterly*, 11(1): 109–127.

Roberts, J. (2003) The manufacture of corporate social responsibility: Constructing corporate sensibility. *Organization*, 10(2): 249–265.

Shamir, R. (2008) The age of responsibilization: On market-embedded morality. *Economy and Society*, 37(1): 1–19.

Shildrick, M. (1997) *Leaky Bodies and Boundaries: Feminism, Postmodernism and (Bio)ethics*. London: Routledge.

ten Bos, R., and Willmott, H. (2001) Towards a post-dualistic business ethics: Interweaving reason and emotion in working life. *Journal of Management Studies*, 38(6): 769–793.

Thanem, T., and Wallenberg, L. (2015). What can bodies do? Reading Spinoza for an affective ethics of organizational life. *Organization*, 22(2): 235–250.

Tyler, M. (2019) Reassembling difference? Rethinking inclusion through/as embodied ethics. *Human Relations*, 72(1): 48–68.

Vachhani, S.J., and Pullen, A. (2019) Ethics, politics and feminist organizing: Writing feminist infrapolitics and affective solidarity into everyday sexism. *Human Relations*, 72(1): 23–47.

Vogel, D. (2008) Private global business regulation. *Annual Review of Political Science*, 11: 261–282.

3 Ethics beyond organizational patriarchy

Corporeal ethics in organizations is taken up through resistance to oppression, discrimination, inequality, and exploitation, especially through collective ethico-political struggles for justice, recognition, and self-determination. This ethics is not commonly instigated by organizations themselves, as represented by those people within them who hold positions of authority. Instead, the ethico-politics that emanates from corporeal ethics is a form of democratic ethics where people come together in intercorporeal relations of embodied care to disrupt and reformulate organizational practices that negate difference. This is a very different ethics to that of dominant approaches to the ethics of organization whose aim is to manage and control the behaviour of others as a putative guarantor of corporate righteousness.

In Chapter 1 we situated corporeal ethics with research and theory in the ethics of organization, in this chapter we contrast it with the way that ethics is explicitly incorporated into organizational discourse and practice – what we refer to as 'corporate ethics'. In so doing, we seek to further distinguish corporeal ethics by examining how it relates to conventional ways that organizations incorporate and justify the idea of the ethics in their actions. In particular, we look at how organizational practices and programmes that are described and justified in ethical terms do not always have ethics (insofar as it is conceived as being other-oriented) as their primary content or rationale. Notably, there are a range of organizational, mainly corporate, practices that seek to associate themselves with ethics and the language of ethics (Painter-Morland, 2015; Rhodes, 2016). Key dimensions of this nominally ethical practice that attract critical attention include: business ethics (e.g. Jones, 2003), corporate social responsibility (e.g. Banerjee, 2008), ethical decision making (e.g. Clegg et al., 2007), corporate codes of ethics (e.g. Jensen et al., 2009), social reporting (e.g. Deegan, 2002), sustainability (e.g. Livesey and

DOI: 10.4324/9781003031048-3

Kearins, 2002), corporate governance (e.g. Roberts, 2001), and corporate environmentalism (Phillips, 2014).

The chapter provides a critical overview of these forms of ethics, focusing mainly on the different motives that corporations can have when they engage in ostensibly ethical practice. This shows how, whether it is used to garner direct commercial advantage, to enhance impression management, or to secure political legitimacy, when business organizations engage in ethics they do so with the primary purpose of the pursuit of self-interest.

Corporate ethics, thus practised, is an ethics that, at its extreme is egocentric, self-serving, and self-glorifying, born as it is out of strategic calculability that engages with others only for what it achieves for the self (Jones, 2003; Bevan and Corvellac, 2007; Rhodes, 2016). Moreover, whether this is ethical in anything but tokenistic terms has been questioned on the basis that 'an ethical choice that can be justified by instrumental gain is not an ethical choice to begin with' (Driver, 2006: 338).

Corporeal ethics as enacted through ethico-politics can include resistance to self-interested practices of organizational ethics as they present as a wolf in sheep's clothing. Corporate ethics, as it is conceived and practised, is masculine and patriarchal and surfacing this reveals its limitations. On this basis, the corporeal ethics of organization is a counterpoint to those corporate ethics that serve to glorify corporations in the interests of regenerating, preserving, and expanding their power. In this sense, the resistance that is central to the ethico-political uptake of corporeal ethics is also a resistance to organizational patriarchy.

The ethics of corporate ethics

Although corporeal ethics is borne out of care and respect for others and their differences, the practice of organizational ethics – especially in corporations – has come under severe scrutiny on account of it being inherently self-regarding. 'Corporate ethics' (Rhodes, 2016) puts self-interest on top of the agenda, when 'discourses of corporate citizenship, social responsibility and sustainability [...] defined by narrow business interests [...] serve to curtail interests of external stakeholders' (Banerjee, 2008: 52) by creating a 'false impression of the firm and legitimate its activities by demonstrating how ethical they are' (Hanlon and Fleming, 2009: 945).

Most directly, organizations can engage in practices associated with ethics to secure direct commercial advantage. So-called ethical initiatives are subjected to a 'business case' (Vogel, 2006) logic: they are only adopted if it can be demonstrated a priori that they will enhance commercial outcomes in the form of, for example, profitability, competitive advantage, or growth. At best the hope is for a 'win-win paradigm' where it is assumed that ethically based results will indubitably be accompanied by favourable financial outcomes (Hahn et al., 2010). Despite this assumption, however, it is the business side of the 'winning' that has been shown to retain the most weight when it comes to decision making. Hence, the 'business case approach results in opportunism, [...] leaves institutional blockades intact and drives out [...] intrinsic motivation' (Nijhof and Jeurissen, 2010: 618).

Consideration of the 'business case for ethics' has led to the conclusion that despite the discussion of mutual benefits, corporations adopt ethics for strategic business purposes without genuine concern for mutuality (Fernández-Kranz and Santaló, 2010). The issue raised through this line of critique is that when ethics is used as a form of corporate strategy, what is deemed as being 'good' is limited only to what is good for business (Banerjee, 2008). In other words, there is no intrinsic or other-focused reason for corporations to behave ethically or responsibly (Scherer and Palazzo, 2007).

From the perspective of corporeal ethics connected to generosity (Diprose, 2002), it is of considerable concern if organizations engage in what are seen as ethical practices 'only to the extent that it makes business sense for them to do so' (Vogel, 2006 4). Despite this, the instrumental approach that uses ethics for direct commercial gain is the one that dominates both theory and practice (Jones, 2009). As with any other form of surplus motivated business activity, if the ethical investment amounts to less than the return in profitability and market dominance, then a 'good' business decision has been made. Ethics is reduced in status to being a commodity and a commercial tool (Shamir, 2008).

Even though the business case approach shows organizations directly and explicitly yoking ethics to commercial self-interest, this connection is more subtle when ethics becomes a form of 'impression management' (Solomon et al., 2013). This management is designed to sustain a myth of ethical accountability while having little or no real effect on the prioritization of financial over ethical concerns (Solomon et al., 2013). With impression management, the focus on 'ethical visibility': 'an essentially self-preoccupied concern with being seen to be being ethical' (Roberts, 2001: 125; Brammer and Millington, 2006). From a more general perspective of business ethics this can involve corporate greenwashing (Laufer, 2003), corporate social responsibility marketing (Jahdi and Acikdilli, 2009), ethical self-aggrandizement (Fleming et al.,

2013), and the deployment of ethics in business is said to secure the public legitimacy of the corporation (Deegan, 2002; Banerjee, 2008). More specifically to organizational ethics can involve implementing corporate ethical codes of conduct which are communicated as an exercise in public relations (Munro, 1992; Frankental, 2001). The focus on impression management suggests that a significant dimension of why corporations engage in ethics is because it is a useful tool for the creation of a socially valued organizational identity. Such ethics is not employed on account of a sense of moral responsibility or a result of moral reasoning, but rather because it results in good publicity in reaction, for example, to external pressure groups (L'Etang, 1994). Creating an impression of being ethical allows corporations to continue with their main activities, especially those that have negative consequences for others, behind the veneer of ethical 'window dressing' or 'white washing' (Painter-Morland, 2006). Using the language of ethics in self-interested business practice has been referred to as an 'ethics of narcissus' (Roberts, 2003) that evinces a preoccupation with looking good in the eyes of others in order to achieve ethically dispassionate corporate goals. Such business ethics is of value to corporations because 'given the grave concerns raised about the conduct of business, talking about ethics may make consumers, customers and shareholders happier to deal with particular companies and their boards' (Sampford and Wood, 1992: 57).

Using ethics for impression management is said to have escalated with companies 'proclaiming the virtues of their ethicality on a scale never before seen' such that 'the very discourse of "ethics", "shared value" and "giving back" to society proliferate in scale, scope and ambition' (Fleming et al., 2013: 339). Such phenomena can be understood to be located in a 'politics of visibility' where corporations actively choose what remains visible and what remains hidden so as to encourage a 'perception of accountability and transparency' (Zyglidopoulos and Fleming, 2011: 702). The purpose is to ensure that one looks good rather than acting and reflecting on what it might mean to be good. Moreover, the emphasis on the appearance of ethical visibility is argued to result in the concealment of 'socially unacceptable behaviour' (p. 692). This concealment works not just to aggrandize the corporation for the sake of aggrandizement, but rather it is an 'ideological tool designed to cloak (or "green wash") an otherwise uncaring corporation in the garb of ethicality and environmental friendliness' (Fleming et al., 2013: 340). In this sense, ethics enables corporations to pursue socially unacceptable self-interested business practices by rendering them less visible to public scrutiny.

On an even broader level, it has been argued that organizations use ethics to gain political legitimacy and regulatory independence. In this case, the ethics that businesses engage in are understood as a form of voluntary self-regulation positioned as a viable substitute for state-based regulation (Marens, 2013), thus enabling corporations to limit social and legal sanction (Matten and Moon, 2008). The development of this form of self-regulation ties in with the more general growth of the power of large corporations under neoliberalism since the 1980s (Carroll and Shabana, 2010). Historically a key juncture was the widespread market deregulation that occurred, initially in the United States and United Kingdom, in the 1980s, as well as forms of reregulation instituted to support global competition (Morgan and Knights, 1997).

This period saw the instantiation of the 'Washington Consensus': a broad politico-economic agreement promulgated by the United States, the European Union, the International Monetary Fund, and the World Bank that 'held that good economic performance required liberalized trade, macroeconomic stability, and getting prices right [... and that...] private markets would produce efficient allocations and growth' (Stiglitz, 1999: 11). Central was market deregulation such that free trade could flourish without the encumbrance of an interventionist state. At this time waves of deregulation and privatization occurred across the world's largest industries (most especially banking and finance, energy, higher education, and transport) together with the freeing up of cross border trade restrictions. These changes privileged the free market as the best way of organizing economic affairs on a global scale. This included a new focus was on 'self-regulative practices based on principles of "diversification" and "increased competition" as an alternative to the old model of top-down, one size fits all, coercive regulation' (Shamir, 2008: 7).

Corporate ethics came into play as a self-regulatory substitute for regulation by government. This was tied up in response to a series of corporate 'disasters' that created renewed calls for regulation. Special attention to the limits of corporate self-regulation was generated by, for example, the leaking of toxic gas from Union Carbide's Bhopal plant in 1984, and The Exxon Valdez oil spill in 1989, as well as, sometime later, the high profile corporate collapses of the Enron Corporation in the United States in 2002 and Parmalat SpA in Europe in 2003. It has been argued that:

> the rise of more socially-responsible corporate behaviour can be interpreted as a response to increasingly well-organized

anti-corporate campaigns, which have been spurred on by the possibilities of global scale coalition-building, and have targeted in particular the worst (or at least the most visible) excesses of corporate exploitation over issues such as labour standards, workplace conditions, and environmental impacts.

(Sadler and Lloyd, 2009: 613)

Moreover, 'in a relaxed legal environment, competitive pressures and market demand and supply become the only key drivers of corporate behavior, which could have negative social outcomes' (Banerjee, 2008: 58). Corporate ethics is positioned as a means through which corporations can claim to buttress themselves against being blamed for these outcomes. The intention, however, is less about genuine ethical matters and more about warding off actual and potential state intervention (Edward and Willmott, 2013). The heart of this line of critique is that corporations use ethics to promote their own regulatory freedoms, so that they can pursue their objectives unencumbered by socio-political interference. This is, in effect, the broader sphere of business ethics as well as in the more specific arena of the ethics of organization.

This contention has been presented recently through debates on what has come to be known as 'Political Corporate Social Responsibility'. Political CSR refers to the ways that increasingly powerful multinational corporations are no longer 'just addressees of regulation but also authors of rules with public impact [...resulting in...] embedding of the corporation in democratic processes of defining rules and tackling global political challenges' (Scherer and Palazzo, 2007: 1098). When this is the case, it is no longer just that corporations evade regulation. More potently, they are positioned as being able to directly influence the regulations that remain. The point is that 'western MNCs are motivated to generate considerable (if not outright maximal) shareholder returns, and that the various political activities they engage in are predominantly informed by instrumental reasoning' (Whelan, 2012: 710). Critically, they do so with little or no 'interest in furthering democracy' (Fleming and Jones, 2012: 45). This is not surprising given that corporations have legal obligations to pursue profitability on behalf of shareholders. That corporate ethics is positioned as having a different purpose to this, while suggestive of a certain hypocrisy, is still consistent with corporate fiduciary duties (see Rhodes and Fleming, 2020).

Focusing on corporate political independence reflects a more complex relationship between corporate ethics and corporate self-interest. The political role of corporations is still in the service of commercial goals such that 'to regard the corporation as a political player whose legitimacy is based on civil society discourses does not mean that corporations should completely transcend the economic logic' (Palazzo and Scherer, 2006: 82). The relationship, however, is one where society places limits on actual and potential profitability both through laws and through a shifting set of cultural norms such that 'corporations consider these rules and the expectations of powerful stakeholder groups as economic restrictions in their course towards maximizing profits' (ibid: 72). In this way, corporate ethics serves to manage and adjust to those restrictions but to do so primarily for economic self-interest.

Gendered ethics

As we have seen above, the way that organizations engage with ethics is closely related to, and supportive of, furthering their commercial self-interest. Therefore, corporate ethics is engaged 'for the purposes of safeguarding the interests of the corporation, rather than a result of a concern for safeguarding certain values or protecting certain rights' (Painter-Morland, 2015: 335). Corporeal ethics of organization is very much at odds with this corporate ethics. The ethico-politics that corporeal ethics tends to is one that would resist corporate ethics, given its support of the 'narrow self-interest of the financial elite' (Banerjee, 2008: 75) at the expense of others.

To advance corporeal ethics for organizations we turn to feminist organization theory and how it explores organizations' gendered and embodied character (Acker, 1990; Britton, 2000; Britton and Logan, 2008; Williams et al., 2012). This work provides a gendered understanding of the reasons that self-interest is valued. It also explains the character of the self that holds those interests. It is well established that business organizations have a gendered substructure (Acker, 1990) that remains hidden through the normalization of a masculine-rational ideal (Phillips et al., 2013) and through the self-interest-based justifications for organizational action that are predicated on it. This normalization is achieved through 'masculine discourses [which] privilege instrumental rationalities that reflect and reinforce an effective attainment of ends through an efficient application of means' (Knights and Kerfoot, 2004: 437).

Gendered theorizing that understands gender as a dimension of organizations (Britton and Logan, 2008) provides a way to see beyond and beneath purely seeing instrumental ends as an explanation in its own right. This points to the productive possibility of considering how the organizational logic of instrumental rationality embedded in corporate ethics exercises power by hiding gendered realities (Ross-Smith and Kornberger, 2004). The exercise of corporate power cannot be so limited that an understanding of it comes to an end with reference to legally sanctioned self-interest; it also reflects long held cultural practices of the glorification of power for its own sake (Agamben, 2011). Establishing a gendered theorization of ethics *and* exploring the non-rational desires that underpin the instrumental corporate engagement with ethics provide a means to differentiate corporeal ethics.

The point is that while organizational engagement in ethics is justified for reasons of financial gain or legitimacy, this justification is structured to garner its value and meaning through enhancing the glory of the corporation and business more generally. Gendered critique is central to understanding this in that the corporation that is glorified by ethics is one cast in a masculine image. This is a trajectory that seeks to probe and problematize how the very ideas that justify corporate ethics are masculine and patriarchal, such that corporeal ethics associated with love, care, and affectual relationships is castigated as being feminine and at best secondary to life in corporations. It is questioning the masculine foundation of the corporation that is central to the development of corporeal ethics. Acknowledging this, dominant practices of ethics in organizations can be theorized in relation to the subordination of 'substantive, ethical, human values and ends' to a 'calculating rationality' (Bologh, 1990: 122). Thus, corporeal ethics of organization can be extended through destabilizing the ethical glorification of the corporation, and displacing its masculinist privilege.

Formal organizations have long privileged 'manly greatness [that] requires restraint, rationality and responsibility' as informed by values of rivalry, action, and strength (Bologh, 1990: 80) and connecting ethics to self-interest is intrinsically tied up in this. If the historical constitution of masculinity involves power and authority being attached to male bodies (Bederman, 2008), then modern corporations can be expected to contain their own modes of attachment. In this fashion, corporate masculinity is said to garner power through its prioritization of 'toughness, strength, conquest and domination' (Eisler, 1991: 6; Van Wensveen, 1995). It is therefore unsurprising that there is a dominant view that 'ethics initiatives will have questionable legitimacy in masculine cultures unless they can be said to contribute to performance' and rest on 'masculine legitimizing rhetoric (e.g. "good ethics is good business")' (Weaver, 2001: 9). Corporate ethics is entrapped in the nexus of commercial self-interest and homosocial masculinity, both of which endorse, perform, and reproduce values associated with autonomy, instrumental rationality, and self-interest (Knights and Tullberg, 2012). Hence, while 'the absence of the feminine persists within even the critical study of business ethics' (Kenny and Fotaki, 2014: 5), its introduction can be used to question and problematize the relation between ethics, self-interest, and instrumental rationality.

Corporate ethics involves idealizing this self as a sovereign patriarchal figure of power (Eisenstein, 1998) whose authority becomes essentialized through this patriarchal positioning (cf. Grosz, 1990) and moral authority. Corporate ethics is thus the servant of the sovereign, corporate patriarch, always at hand to glorify the master. The power that can be wielded and desired by corporate ethics far exceeds the pursuit of financial self-interest; it is also related to modelling the corporation on a male God. We note from our earlier discussion that corporate ethics is often a matter of public visibility, more about outward and socially noticeable displays of ethicality than inward reflection, interpersonal closeness, and love. This is an ethics of the public realm that 'has continued to be associated symbolically with the masculine, and the private with the feminine' (Jaggar, 2000: 455). Further, the privatization of what is rendered other to the masculine becomes feminized within a masculine discourse of corporate ethics.

A masculine drive for public greatness is at the heart of a corporation when it vies for glory for itself in a public world of market-based rivalry. Present is a powerful image of the corporate self-rooted in a masculinity that relies on ruthlessness, aggressiveness, competition, and adversarialness for its meaning (Acker, 2004). The 'outer world of conflict, competition and striving' that characterizes corporate masculinity is part of a 'patriarchal model of manliness' (Bologh, 1990: 245) the achievement of which can only be reached through the 'image of a strong man who is dependent on no one' (p. 14). What we have here is a particular religiously infused image of masculinity connected as it is to what Weber identifies as the puritan ethic of capitalism. Valued is an asceticism that establishes masculine independence forged by the application of rationality yet does so 'out of a devotion to a higher cause' (Bologh, 1990: 223). This higher cause is the mode of corporate sovereignty (Barkan, 2013) whereby it is the corporation whose greatness and righteousness means that it is at the apex of the trinity: sovereign, independent, assertive, and beyond reproach.

Corporate ethics can be now understood to function to glorify the corporate self as patriarch as well as to glorify patriarchy. Importantly, this enactment of patriarchy concerns the organization of sovereign power itself. The sovereignty associated with masculine self-sufficient independence requires a renunciation of paternal love (Bologh, 1990) such that the ideal man is the one who no longer needs a father. Similarly what demands investigation is how, in the context of neoliberalism, corporate ethics can free (or at least attempt to free) the corporation from the paternalism of the state, with the added sting of rendering the corporation itself as the *pater*. As the new patriarch, the corporation is the one who assumes the role of the protector: the supreme being who can look after 'him' self and after others, but who does not require any looking after by anyone else. This is masculinity at its powerful and dangerous apex. It is masculinity so pure that it has freed itself from external judgement or sanction over its sovereign actions. Glorified in its righteousness, the corporation would be the custodian and judge of morality; it would require no Father and thus is the supreme man in whose image lowly flesh and blood men are made.

As our discussion intimates, the value of examining corporate ethics in relation to patriarchy lies not just in its descriptive or analytical purchase, but also so in that it can castigate assumedly feminine and private matters of love, relationality, and care as being either outside of or in service of what is implied as the instrumental purpose business, and of corporate ethics. Corporate ethics, when it works to glorify corporations, is a public matter associated with acclaim, glorification, masculine independence, and potency. When this is the case 'banishing care and nurturance to the private sphere ensures that the public world remains masculine regardless of how many women enter it' (Bologh, 1990: 4; cf. Wajcman, 1998; Knights and Tullberg, 2012; Pullen and Vachhani, 2020). That this can occur through the signifier 'ethics' however is not a minor or incidental matter. When corporate ethics is about masculine power and its glorification, invoking this glorification through the term *ethics* is significant and ambiguous.

The patriarchal masculinity supported by the public glorification of corporations excludes the feminine, if not excluding actual women, from public, especially corporate, life (cf. Knights and Tullberg, 2012). There is a gendered bifurcation of values at play based on the assumption that corporeal values of care for others, nurturance, and generosity are matters for the feminine private sphere of the home, with the masculine public spheres of politics and economy being places suited to instrumental rationality and directed action (Gatens, 1996). Values that do not conform to masculine instrumental rationality are thus 'external to the logic of political economy' because they are inimical to 'a world in which conflict and struggles for power continue because it is out of conflict that strengths are developed and greatness achieved' (Bologh, 1990:

274–275). It is in this way that instrumental rationality, conceit, and assumed independence can be questioned in relation to the possibility that corporations do not need to disavow the prospect of being 'devoted to the Other before being devoted to itself' (Chalier, 1991: 126). This is quite the opposite of manly greatness, sovereignty, and self-glorification in that it 'encompasses connectivity, inclusivity and compassion' as a means to respond ethically to others (Kenny and Fotaki, 2014: 2). Corporeal ethics is thus excluded from the patriarchal organization.

It is noteworthy that business discourse has adopted the term *ethics*: a matter, in some of its senses, understood as personal and private, suitable for issues concerning interpersonal relations and other interactions belonging in the private sphere; the assumedly feminine sphere. Justice, as a more rational and public notion, could have been used such that so-called '"feminine" concerns with the personal and particular' could be totally overtaken with masculine impartiality and the 'abstract character of reason' (Lloyd, 1993: 106). But no, it is *ethics*, a term whose originary meaning has been associated with the 'epiphany of the feminine' (Levinas, 1969: 245). The language of corporate ethics is replete with allusions that at first glance seem to defy, or at least ambiguate, the masculinity of which we have been accusing it. We have notions such as the 'caring corporation' (Livesey and Kearins, 2002) wrapped up cosily in the context of a capitalism that itself can be caring (Barman, 2016) and compassionate. Again, with corporate ethics we see values associated with the private feminized sphere being used in the context of business hand in hand with the values of greatness, conquest, and achievement.

Our discussion so far has asserted the distinct masculinity of corporate ethics as it relates to corporate power through public glorification of the corporate self as patriarch. How then can we account for the feminine significations ethics avers? Considering this question, we take care in recognizing that a feminine rendering of ethics has a distinct relationship with masculinity; a relationship that is internal to patriarchy. The idea of a feminine ethics serves to privilege the primacy of the masculine perspective in the act of revering the feminine (De Beauvoir, 1949) as if placed on an ethical pedestal to be objectified within the masculine gaze, and in so doing nourishing the masculine position (Irigaray, 1991; Perpich, 2001; Ziarek, 2001). Accordingly, the corporate masculinity enabled by corporate ethics is not so much a rejection of the feminine, but more a co-optation of it for the purpose of masculine public glory. By analogy, corporate ethics is busy cleaning, so that when the man of the house comes home, he regales himself in the sparkling glory of all that falls under his dominion. It is not the ethics that matters, other than that it supports the visibility of greatness.

The meaning of corporate ethics is one where the feminine is not absent but instead is rendered as being at the service of the masculine, the latter being understood in relation to domination, greatness, and sovereignty. As such, in the conception and practice of corporate ethics, the feminine is simultaneously privileged, incorporated, and silenced; it is the little woman of the manly corporation. Corporate ethics extinguishes the agency of the feminine by rendering it always in need of and in service to the masculine; it becomes further enshrined as the glorification of masculinity in a corporate form, achieved with the support of the image of a loving, docile and subservient woman. It would seem that the cliché 'behind every great man there stands a woman' is realized, in extremis, in corporate ethics.

Ways forward

In bringing this chapter to a close, we acknowledge that imagining a different ethics that responds to the reality of corporations 'cannot be reduced to exposing the failures, arbitrariness, and hypocrisies of those who would affiliate themselves with sovereign authority (the pater) in hopes of ascending to a decision-making role within a given community' (Galewski, 2008: 397). To do so would be tantamount to demanding that one mode of patriarchal domination be replaced with another that better suits one's own interests and preferences. Moreover, our critique of corporate ethics is not meant to suggest that corporeal ethical acts based on a genuine care and concerns for other people do not go on in corporations. Such things happen every day, but although people in corporations might genuinely be motivated by a desire to serve others, this does not change how corporate ethics, as an organized and managed set of corporate activities, relates to corporate self-interest.

Corporate ethics is an incorporation of ethics: a bringing in, assimilation and appropriation. With ethics thus incorporated the requirement for singular uniformity takes hold. Ethics, as far as corporate ethics is concerned, must conform to, and support the logic of the system to which it is brought in. Corporeal ethics of organization goes beyond the conclusion that ethics is simply a means through which corporations pursue economic self-interest. This means acknowledging the dominance of masculine-rational economic self-interest as a starting point for ethical critique, as well as other-focused resistance. It is this resistance that we explore in the next chapter.

References

Acker, J. (1990) Hierarchies, jobs, bodies: A theory of gendered organizations. *Gender and Society*, 4(2): 139–158.

Acker, J. (2004) Gender, capitalism and globalization. *Critical Sociology*, 30(1): 17–41.

Agamben, G. (2011) *The Kingdom and the Glory: For a Theological Genealogy of Economy and Government.* Stanford, CA: Stanford University Press.

Banerjee, S.B. (2008) Corporate social responsibility: The good, the bad and the ugly. *Critical Sociology*, 34(1): 51–79.

Barkan, J. (2013) *Corporate Sovereignty: Law and Government Under Capitalism.* Minneapolis: University of Minnesota Press.

Barman, E. (2016) *Caring Capitalism.* Cambridge: Cambridge University Press.

Bederman, G. (2008) *Manliness and Civilization: A Cultural History of Gender and Race in the United States, 1880–1917.* Chicago, IL: University of Chicago Press.

Bevan, D., and Corvellec, H. (2007) The impossibility of corporate ethics: For a Levinasian approach to managerial ethics. *Business Ethics: a European Review*, 16(3): 208–219.

Bologh, R.W. (1990) *Love or Greatness: Max Weber and Masculine Thinking: A Feminist Inquiry.* London: Unwin Hyman.

Brammer, S., and Millington, A. (2006) Firm size, organizational visibility and corporate philanthropy: An empirical analysis. *Business Ethics: A European Review*, 15(1): 6–18.

Britton, D.M. (2000) The epistemology of the gendered organization. *Gender & Society*, 14(3): 418–434.

Britton, D.M., and Logan, L. (2008) Gendered organizations: Progress and prospects. *Sociology Compass*, 2(1): 107–121.

Carroll, A.B., and Shabana, K.M. (2010) The business case for corporate social responsibility: A review of concepts, research and practice. *International Journal of Management Reviews*, 12(1): 85–105.

Chalier, C. (1991) Ethics and the feminine. In R. Bernasconi and S. Critchley (Eds.), pp. 119–129, *Re-reading Levinas.* Bloomington: Indiana University Press.

Clegg, S., Kornberger, M., and Rhodes, C. (2007) Organizational ethics, decision making, undecidability. *The Sociological Review*, 55(2): 393–409.

De Beauvoir, S. (1949) *The Second Sex.* London: Vintage.

Deegan, C. (2002) Introduction: The legitimizing effect of social and environmental disclosures—A theoretical foundation. *Accounting, Auditing & Accountability Journal*, 15(3): 282–311.

Diprose, R. (2002) *Corporeal Generosity: On Giving with Nietzsche, Merleau-Ponty and Levinas.* New York: State University of New York Press.

Driver, M. (2006) Beyond the stalemate of economics versus ethics: Corporate social responsibility and the discourse of the organizational self. *Journal of Business Ethics*, 66(4): 337–356.

Edward, P., and Willmott, H. (2013) Discourse and normative business ethics. In C. Luetge (Ed.), pp. 549–580, *Handbook of the Philosophical Foundations of Business Ethics*. Dordrecht: Springer.

Eisenstein, Z.R. (1998) *Global Obscenities: Patriarchy, Capitalism, and the Lure of Cyberfantasy*. New York: New York University Press.

Eisler, R. (1991) Women, men, and management: Redesigning our future. *Futures*, 23(1): 3–18.

Fernández-Kranz, D., and Santaló, J. (2010) When necessity becomes a virtue: The effect of product market competition on corporate social responsibility. *Journal of Economics and Management Strategy*, 19(2): 453–487.

Fleming, P., and Jones, M.T. (2012) *The End of Corporate Social Responsibility: Crisis and Critique*. London: Sage.

Fleming, P., Roberts, J., and Garsten, C. (2013) In search of corporate social responsibility. *Organization*, 20(3): 337–348.

Frankental, P. (2001) Corporate social responsibility – A PR invention? *Corporate Communications: An International Journal*, 6(1): 18–23.

Galewski, E. (2008) Foundering to me is sweet in this sea: Agamben's theory of ethical life. *Review of Communication*, 8(4): 395–404.

Gatens, M. (1996) *Imaginary Bodies: Ethics, Power and Corporeality*. London: Routledge.

Grosz, E. (1990) Conclusion: A note of essentialism and difference. In S.M. Gunew (Ed.), pp. 332–344, *Feminist Knowledge: Critique and Construct*. London: Routledge.

Hahn, T., Figge, F., Pinkse, J., and Preuss, L. (2010) Trade-offs in corporate sustainability: You can't have your cake and eat it. *Business Strategy and the Environment*, 19(4): 217–229.

Hanlon, G., and Fleming, P.P. (2009) Updating the critical perspective on corporate social responsibility. *Sociology Compass*, 3(6): 937–948.

Irigaray, L. (1991) Questions to Emmanuel Levinas: On the divinity of love. In R. Bernasconi and S. Critchley (Eds.), pp. 109–118, *Re-Reading Levinas*. Bloomington: Indiana University Press.

Jaggar, A.M. (2000) Ethics naturalized: Feminism's contribution to moral epistemology. *Metaphilosophy*, 31(5): 452–468.

Jahdi, K.S., and Acikdilli, G. (2009) Marketing communications and corporate social responsibility (CSR): Marriage of convenience or shotgun wedding? *Journal of Business Ethics*, 88(1): 103–113.

Jensen, T., Sandström, J., and Helin, S. (2009) Corporate codes of ethics and the bending of moral space. *Organization*, 16(4): 529–545.

Jones, C. (2003) As if business ethics were possible, 'within such limits'... *Organization*, 10(2): 223–248.

Jones, M.T. (2009) Disrobing the emperor: Mainstream CSR research and corporate hegemony. *Management of Environmental Quality: An International Journal*, 20(3): 335–346.

Kenny, K., and Fotaki, M. (2014) From gendered organizations to compassionate borderspaces: Reading corporeal ethics with Bracha Ettinger. *Organization*, 22(2): 183–199.

Knights, D., and Kerfoot, D. (2004). Between representations and subjectivity: Gender binaries and the politics of organizational transformation. *Gender, Work & Organization*, 11(4): 430–454.

Knights, D., and Tullberg, M. (2012) Managing masculinity/mismanaging the corporation. *Organization*, 19(4): 385–404.

Laufer, W.S. (2003) Social accountability and corporate greenwashing. *Journal of Business Ethics*, 43(3): 253–261.

L'Etang, J. (1994) Public relations and corporate social responsibility: Some issues arising. *Journal of Business Ethics*, 13(2): 111–123.

Levinas, E. (1969) *Totality and Infinity: An Essay on Exteriority.* Pittsburgh, PA: Duquesne University Press.

Livesey, S.M., and Kearins, K. (2002) Transparent and caring corporations? A study of sustainability reports by the Body Shop and Royal Dutch/Shell. *Organization and Environment*, 15(3): 233–258.

Lloyd, G. (1993) *The Man of Reason: 'Male' and 'Female' in Western Philosophy*, 2nd ed. London: Routledge.

Marens, R. (2013) What comes around: The early 20th century American roots of legitimating corporate social responsibility. *Organization*, 20(3), 454–476.

Matten, D., and Moon, J. (2008) 'Implicit' and 'explicit' CSR: A conceptual framework for a comparative understanding of corporate social responsibility. *Academy of Management Review*, 33(2): 404–424.

Morgan, G., and Knights, D. (Eds.) (1997) *Deregulation and European Financial Services.* London: Macmillan.

Munro, I. (1992) Codes of ethics. Some uses and abuses. In P. Davies (Ed.), pp. 97–106, *Current Issues in Business Ethics.* London: Routledge.

Nijhof, A.H.J., and Jeurissen, R.J.M. (2010) The glass ceiling of corporate social responsibility: Consequences of a business case approach towards CSR. *International Journal of Sociology and Social Policy*, 30(11/12): 618–631.

Painter-Morland, M. (2006) Triple bottom-line reporting as social grammar: Integrating corporate social responsibility and corporate codes of conduct. *Business Ethics: A European Review*, 15(4): 352–364.

Painter-Morland, M. (2015) A critical analysis of ethics management practices. In A. Pullen and C. Rhodes (Eds.), pp. 335–351, *The Routledge Companion to Ethics, Politics and Organizations.* London: Routledge.

Palazzo, G., and Scherer, A. G. (2006) Corporate legitimacy as deliberation: A communicative framework. *Journal of Business Ethics*, 66(1): 71–88.

Perpich, D. (2001) From the caress to the word: Transcendence and the feminine in the philosophy of Emmanuel Levinas. In T. Chanter (Ed.), pp. 28–52, *Feminist Interpretations of Emmanuel Levinas.* Pittsburgh, University Park: The Pennsylvania State University Press.

Phillips, M. (2014) Re-writing corporate environmentalism: Ecofeminism, corporeality and the language of feeling. *Gender, Work & Organization*, 21(5): 443–458.

Phillips, M., Pullen, A., and Rhodes, C. (2013) Writing organization as gendered practice: Interrupting the libidinal economy. *Organization Studies*, 35(3): 313–333.

Pullen, A., and Vachhani, S.J. (2020) Feminist ethics and women leaders: From difference to intercorporeality. *Journal of Business Ethics*, https://doi.org/10.1007/s10551-020-04526-0

Rhodes, C. (2016) Democratic business ethics: Volkswagen's emissions scandal and the disruption of corporate sovereignty. *Organization Studies*, 37(10): 1501–1518.

Rhodes, C., and Fleming, P. (2020). Forget political corporate social responsibility. *Organization*, 27(6): 943–951.

Roberts, J. (2001) Corporate governance and the ethics of narcissus. *Business Ethics Quarterly*, 11(1): 109–127.

Roberts, J. (2003) The manufacture of corporate social responsibility: Constructing corporate sensibility. *Organization*, 10(2): 249–265.

Ross-Smith, A., and Kornberger, M. (2004) Gendered rationality? A genealogical exploration of the philosophical and sociological conceptions of rationality, masculinity and organization. *Gender, Work and Organization*, 11(3): 280–305.

Sadler, D., and Lloyd, S. (2009) Neo-liberalising corporate social responsibility: A political economy of corporate citizenship, *Geoforum*, 40: 613–622.

Sampford, C., and Wood, D. (1992) Future of business ethics-legal regulation, ethical standard setting and institutional design. *The Griffith Law Review*, 1(1): 56–72.

Scherer, A.G., and Palazzo, G. (2007) Toward a political conception of corporate responsibility: Business and society seen from a Habermasian perspective. *Academy of Management Review*, 32(4): 1096–1120.

Shamir, R. (2008) The age of responsibilization: On market-embedded morality. *Economy and Society*, 37(1): 1–19.

Solomon, J.F., Solomon, A., Joseph, N.L., and Norton, S.D. (2013) Impression management, myth creation and fabrication in private social and environmental reporting: Insights from Erving Goffman. *Accounting, Organizations and Society*, 38(3): 195–213.

Stiglitz, J.E. (1999) More instruments and broader goals: Moving toward the Post-Washington consensus. *Revista de Economia Política*, 19(1): 94–120.

Van Wensveen, L.M. (1995) Is toughness a business virtue? *International Journal of Applied Philosophy*, 9(2): 15–25.

Vogel, D. (2006) *The Market for Virtue: The Potential and Limits of Corporate Social Responsibility*. Washington, DC: Brookings Institution Press.

Wajcman, J. (1998) *Managing Like a Man: Women and Men in Corporate Management*. Cambridge: Polity.

Weaver, G.R. (2001) Ethics programs in global businesses: Culture's role in managing ethics. *Journal of Business Ethics*, 30(1): 3–15.

Whelan, G. (2012) The political perspective of corporate social responsibility: A critical research agenda. *Business Ethics Quarterly*, 22(04): 709–737.

Williams, C.L., Muller, C., and Kilanski, K. (2012) Gendered organizations in the new economy. *Gender & Society*, 26(4): 549–573.

Ziarek, E. (2001) The ethical passions of Emmanuel Levinas. In T. Chanter (Ed.), pp. 78–95, *Feminist Interpretations of Emmanuel Levinas*. University Park: The Pennsylvania State University Press.

Zyglidopoulos, S., and Fleming, P. (2011) Corporate accountability and the politics of visibility in late modernity. *Organization*, 18(5): 691–706.

4   An ethico-politics of resistance

Corporeal ethics is not a detached ethics that serves as a framework through which people can draw morally righteous conclusions about what to do or who to be. Happening at the sites of everyday interactions and between mutually dependent embodied persons, corporeal ethics is better understood as ethico-politics. This ethico-politics considers possibilities for ethically motivated political action in the name of respecting, preserving, and caring for others and their personal and intersectional differences – differences that are bound by contested socio-cultural hierarchies of domination and subordination. Corporeal ethics both extend the existing conceptions of the ethics of organization and contest the patriarchal corporate ethics that we discussed in the previous chapter. This contestation involves political action against forms of oppression and discrimination that appropriate difference for the purposes of the self or to establish a position of material and political superiority. Corporeal ethics is dedicated to liberating difference. It includes the freedom to be and become oneself and live a life infused with individual and collective empowerment. Further, corporeal ethics also includes the right to critique and resist forces of power and authority that dominate people so as to curtail freedom.

As a political act in and against organizations, resistance has by no means gone unnoticed in the study of organization although, as we shall see, it is generally not explicitly connected to ethics (cf. Foster and Wiebe, 2010; Alakavuklar and Alamgir, 2018; Younes et al., 2020). From our perspective, this is remiss because it is by appreciating the politics of organizational resistance that we can elaborate how corporeal ethics plays out in practice. Since the 1970s there has been much said about resistance in organizations beginning in particular from an engagement with workplace resistance in the labour process (e.g. Burawoy, 1979; Thompson, 1989). In the early 1990s,

DOI: 10.4324/9781003031048-4

however, the dangers of conceptualizing resistance as a general theory were questioned, most especially in the pages of John Jermier et al.'s (1994) edited collection *Resistance and Power in Organisations*. This foundational book in critical studies of organizations problematized the nature of resistance by describing and theorizing specific forms of resistant practices in diverse organizational contexts. Emphasizing 'localised forms of resistance and subjectivity' (1994: 8) the contributors surfaced the power relations at play in organizations and how they can be enacted in specific settings and in specific ways.

A key distinction was advanced by David Collinson (1994) who contrasted 'resistance through persistence' with 'resistance at a distance'. With the latter Collinson was able to discern how less direct (and less observable) forms of resistance against managerial control are performed in relation to the varied subjectivities at play and at stake in workplace power relations. Collinson questioned the belief that what were at the time newer forms of managerial control (based especially on culture and values) had outflanked the potential for resistance among employees (cf. Thompson and Ackroyd, 1995). He did so by examining resistance as it emerged through particular types of relations between organizations and employees. It is this focus on relations, and power relations in particular (Knights and Vurdubakis, 1994), that marks a central trend in contemporary theories of resistance in organizations (Fleming and Spicer, 2003; Mumby, 2005; Ybema et al., 2016; Mumby et al., 2017).

Since the mid-1990s, research into the forms of resistance theorized by Collinson has developed significantly, surfacing the ways that resistance can be covert and subversive (Ackroyd and Thompson, 1999; Fleming and Sewell, 2002; Fleming, 2005) while at the same time problematizing the power-resistance dichotomy (Burrell, 1992; Iedema et al., 2006; Nentwich and Hoyer, 2012). Particular attention has been paid to the ways resistance can be cynical such that what is observable as compliant is not necessarily so in intent (Fleming and Spicer, 2003). This form of resistance is 'inconspicuous, subjective, subtle and unorganised' (Fleming and Sewell, 2002: 859; Younes et al., 2020) in contrast with traditionally more public forms of resistance such as industrial action, overt misbehaviour, whistleblowing, or even occupations (Mumby et al., 2017). Either way, resistance has been studied by examining how it takes place through the relationships between organizational members, most commonly employees resisting forms of managerial control. Such resistance seeks to 'challenge, invert, or disrupt top-down control' of both individuals and groups (Zanin and Bisel, 2020). It surfaces where employees perceive 'that the organisation requires the mere performance of "appropriate behaviour" in conformance with politically correct, managerially fashionable and legalistically expedient expectations', such that resistance can be enacted both through and outside that performance (Westwood and Johnston, 2012: 787). Resistance can also manifest in opposition to managerial action that manifests in forms of domination and coercion (Alcadipani et al., 2018).

Attending to modes of resistance that were 'widespread but under-appreciated' (Jermier et al., 1994: x), there became a greater level of appreciation of 'the ways that employees oppose new managerial regimes, invariably harbouring feelings of resentment and discontent and sometimes even reverse employer initiatives' (Fleming and Sewell, 2002: 658). This shift relied on an appreciation of how power operated on a less formal basis that had previously been assumed. It also relied on an acknowledgement how:

> ... the ubiquitous nature of power does not deny space for resistance since power is neither exhaustive of social relations nor totalising with respect to subjectivity. There are discontinuities, and gaps that leave considerable space for resistance.
>
> (Jermier et al., 1994: 16; see also Townley, 2005)

Within this frame, power relations between an organization's members, especially at the level of ethical subjectivity, can be located (McMurray et al., 2011; Alakavuklar and Alamgir, 2018).

Extending earlier contributions surrounding the relationship between power and resistance, and by drawing on corporeal ethics, we move beyond the established argument that 'resistance might become a visible target, enabling the intensification of discipline and control' (Burrell, 1992 cited in Collinson, 2002: 743). We move towards a conceptualization of resistance as productive (see Fleming, 2007; Knights and McCabe, 2000) and ethically informed (McMurray et al., 2011; Alakavuklar and Alamgir, 2018). We note here that although the privileging of resistance as an area of study has undermined the assumptions that organizations can necessarily direct and control employees at the levels of behaviour and subjectivity (Townley, 2005), this largely does not explicitly consider how this exercise of counter-power might be related to, of informed by, ethics (cf. Parker, 1999; Ball, 2005). Where an implicit ethics can be discerned, it takes the form of how organizational power (that which is to be resisted) might restrict the freedom of employees in their self-formation, a self-righteous struggle against the 'hegemony of management' (Spicer and Böhm, 2007).

Restricting ethics to matters of freedom and self-formation, however, can easily yield a self-focused approach that does not adequately consider the ethical relations with others (Critchley, 2008), an ethics borne of generosity (Diprose, 2002), or collective political action and political solidarity (Montes and Pombo, 2019). This calls for a broader consideration of 'collective ethics of resistance as the view that people should actively participate in the creation and maintenance of their own social relations' rather than them being imposed authoritatively (Courpasson and Marti, 2019: 1).

While questions of 'where, who, when, and how' are asked in relation to resistance (Mumby et al., 2017), the ethical question of 'why' has been less prevalent. This omission calls us to consider the motives and desires behind resisting, the purposes that resistance serves, and who benefits from resistance. Commonly there is a simple and untested assumption that there exists an essential antagonism between workers and capitalist organizations as represented by managers, in a way that limits the experiential contexts and particularities that give rise to specific acts of resistance (McCabe et al., 2020). While not eschewing this as an inherent condition of capitalism, assuming that all resistance arises only out of structural economic conditions fails to account for the agency and subjectivity of those involved in the relations. Moreover, assuming that antagonism is always pre-determined in both its existence and its form risks sanctifying resistance of all kinds without considering the basis on which it is enacted or ethically justified.

An emerging body of research in management and organization studies has extended earlier debates by drawing on feminist theory to place bodies at the centre of ethically informed resistance. This ethics is political in that it is inexorably connected to action for change. Moreover, this is an ethico-politics arising from and mobilized through the affective relations between bodies. Fotaki et al.'s (2014) gendered reading of power and organizational hierarchy develops and exemplifies this approach. It does so through the articulation of a feminist writing of organization that can surface the destructive effects of power in organizations by placing feminine materiality at the centre of resistance. The politics that Fotaki et al. advocate challenges masculine dominance through an affectively charged questioning of the 'taken-for-granted oppressive hierarchical relationships wherever they may occur' (p. 1263). Far from being resistance for the sake of resistance, what Fotaki et al. point to is the necessity of embedded political action to redress historically saturated injustices. They also remind us of the danger of phallic dominance of the feminine when resistance is constructed as a masculine power. This echoes the dangers inherent when the feminine is to be deployed for masculinity glory (Rhodes and Pullen, 2018; Vachhani, 2020), oven when that glory might itself manifest in the assertion of the power of resistance itself.

How we move beyond a reduction and exploitation of the feminine is the focus of a recent contribution to discussions of dissent and ethics, which puts sexual difference at the centre of radical democratic ethics. Sheena Vachhani (2020) analyses the global #MeToo movement and Sisters Uncut (United Kingdom) to suggest that through political activism – and in these cases, women's activism – embodied and situated ethics can emerge. A 'tactical reassertion of difference' (p. 754) becomes key to the resistance of democratic dissent. As Vachhani shows, feminist politics, which begins with the inequalities grounded in sexual difference, is fundamental to ethics. Vachhani's argument is that through a 'democratic culture of difference' the character of the exclusion of the marginalized can be reconceived. Central to this reconceptualization is surfacing the power that sustains inequality, marginalization, and exclusion. Crucially, this reveals how this power can be disrupted on ethical grounds through political action. Through such exercises of power, the feminine (in its intersectionality) can be reimagined in its full potential.

The realization of human potential yields the possibility of a life worth living. Reflecting on the demands placed on people through the COVID-19 crisis, Marjan De Coster (2020) reminds us, relational ethics for living are critical to 'recognising the openness and generosity in the relation' (p. 747). De Coster illustrates this by considering how, for people with responsibilities for caring for children, relational ethics became especially palpable during COVID. What also rose to the surface was the 'ethical burden' created by the co-presence of demands from work and demands to care. For many, if not most, this was a gendered ethical experience. Attending to care, De Coster (2020) argues, 'leverages the constitution of masculine subjectivity, and, so doing, further increases the ontological struggle in the constitution of female subjectivity' (p. 747). In managing this struggle, and in seeking relief from the ethical burden, De Coster turns to how 'relational ethics can finally replace the normative business ethics of exchange, and that an unburdened ethical female subjectivity can emerge' (p.751).

The ethics in resistance

What is implicitly present in the accounts of power and resistance reviewed above is an ethics grounded in the freedom of the individual subject to engage in alternatives to that which they are dominated by or coerced into; an excursion into the 'undecided space' where subjectivity and practice is not beholden to normalizing discourse or practice (Bevir, 1999; Iedema and Rhodes, 2010; Raffnsøe et al., 2019). Considering resistance as embodied as well as discursive enabled us to identify and render explicit how resistance is an ethico-political practice in organizations and of organizing. This is an ethics that seeks to undermine and transform the marginalization and inequality that results from the instantiation of dominant norms and pre-determined relations through organizations' cultures and practices. We are reminded of Collinson's (2005) observation that '[r]esistance itself can [...] be subject to disciplinary responses and power may not only produce, but also shape dissent' (p. 743). Collinson shows that where resistance is merely a matter of pushing back because of not wanting to be pushed, then the consequences can, ironically, be to play into the palm of the pushing hand. Accordingly, Robyn Thomas and Annette Davies (2005) suggest that change is about making a difference that 'refutes the "romanticised" view of power' (p. 720).

In relation to corporeal ethics, this differentiation calls for the engagement of resistance within broader collective political concerns and as they are informed by ethics. Whereas the emphasis on acts of resistance (Fleming and Sewell, 2002), discursive resistance (Fleming and Spicer, 2003), or micro-political resistance (Thomas and Davies, 2005) is important, they can be further elaborated by explicitly accounting for a resistance born of the desire of an ethical engagement in the socio-political context of organizations as located in the embodied relations between people. The intercorporeality of intersectionally diverse bodies containing visible and invisible differences gives rise to contested relations through which ethico-political opportunities arise. The discussions of resistance in organizations canvassed so far share the idea that unequal power relations are questionable because of their direction and confinement of subjectivity and freedom, especially as they relate to employees. The way that such resistance might be founded in a prior ethics remains at best implicit (for exceptions see Alakavuklar and Alamgir, 2018; Courpasson and Marti, 2019). It is in seeking to make this explicit that the practice of corporeal ethics can be productively extended to the study of ethics and organizations. This extension produces an understanding of the relationship between ethics and politics based on corporeal ethics and in contrast to coercive organizational ethics (as seen in Chapter 2) and self-interested corporate ethics (as seen in Chapter 3). Moreover, this further develops our understanding of both ethics and resistance in organizations by placing resistance centre stage in how ethical practice in organizations is conceived.

Ethico-politics is a political practice founded in an ethics of radical embodied generosity that is manifest neither in the 'self serving collection of debts nor in an expectation of unconditional self sacrifice in the service of the other but in the indeterminacy of generous acts that lie somewhere in between' (Diprose, 2002: 187). It is with this political position, that the potential for connecting ethics, politics, and resistance in the study of organizations is possible. This is political in the sense that it relies on understanding power as diffuse and affective such that what is to be resisted is power's proliferation through normalization and institutionalization that serve to 'limit the other through familiar ideas' (p. 137). This calls for generosity and openness as the basis of actual political action; to be meaningful ethics must be mobilized in practical situations, most especially through resistance.

As we have already established, dominant approaches to organizational and corporate ethics locate ethics within organizational practice and managerial behaviour. What ethico-politics adds is a focus on those ethics that are not formulated by an organization, but rather emerge in relation to it (Rhodes, 2016), for example, where 'resistance has ethical content in response to a managerial ethics of compliance and conformity implemented through various control mechanisms in organisations' (Alakavuklar and Alamgir, 2018: 31). Resisting management just because it involves organizing and directing the work of others is, however, an insufficient ethical position, in that it can simply reflect a recalcitrance to authority instigated solely on the basis of a desire to be an anti-authoritarian. Such a reactionary position would resist authority purely because it is authority, rather than on account of adverse effects of the exercise of power on other people's well-being.

With corporeal ethics, attention is drawn not merely to authority per se, but rather to situations where power operates practically to create systems and practices of oppression, discrimination, and exploitation that negate the otherness of the other, noting that that not all exercises of authority do this. Discrimination and inequality as they concern sex, gender, heterosexism, class, race, and nation (as well as the relations between them) are central to what goes on in organizations (Holvino, 2010; Amis et al., 2019; McEwen et al., 2021), and moreover, these are distinctly ethico-political matters. While historically it has been the case that even in critically oriented scholarship of organizations 'there is a dearth of theory and research that has systematically addressed issues of race, sexuality, able-bodiedness, and so forth' (Mumby, 2008: 27; Bell et al., 2019; cf. Pullen et al., 2019), it is a theorization of ethico-politics that points to the ethical criticality of such research. As we elaborated, the translation of ethical generosity into political resistance is made by seeking practical action resist oppression and helps realize social conditions that do not close down, negate, suppress, or normalize difference. This is not to say that organizations are always or necessarily oppressively normalizing, or that management action of all types warrants resistance, but rather that it is the condition of the normalization of difference that gives rise to a politically motivated ethical response of resistance.

If it is the case that organizations are 'dominated by a rationality that eschews [...] generosity as at best, utopian, and at worst economically and culturally subversive' (Hancock, 2008: 1371), how then might this generosity come to bear on organizations? There are no codes of exchange or solid organizational arrangements that can regulate the generosity of the affective body. Corporeal ethics does not start with the collective management of ethics, it consists instead of affectively resisting those organizational norms and practices that perpetuate systems of oppression. Such an ethics 'does not aspire to a neutral position transcending power and embodiment, provided for instance by normative criteria, but rather articulates the difficult role of responsibility and freedom in democratic struggles' (Ziarek, 2001: 4). Moreover, while resistance might be undertaken by single persons, either for the benefit of themselves or for others, its full potential is realized when collectively mobilized for the benefit of others. This ethics gains impact when people come together to respond to 'oppression as a collective project, deriving from an ethical demand for political action' (Courpasson and Marti, 2018: 854).

Care needs to be taken to neither romanticize resistance nor underestimate the challenges it brings. This is not the resistance of the 'subtle subversives who resist from within by cynically acquiescing to the demands of managed work' (Rhodes, 2009: 398) but one that engages with the difficult political challenges demanded by an ethics that refuses to capitulate to oppression by power. Two recent studies serve to illustrate this. The first is David Courpasson and Ignasi Marti's (2018) study of ethically informed resistance by Jewish inhabitants of a Warsaw Ghetto during the Holocaust. During this time direct, explicit, and extreme oppression and persecution of Jews by the Nazis lead millions to their death. The ghettoization of Jews, which Courpasson and Marti's study focused on, involved 'the creation [hundreds] of new social spaces and structures that fully regulated the possession and distribution of goods, privilege, prestige, and ultimately life itself through different practices and regulations [...] a fundamental step in the process of increasing oppression and terror' (p. 860). Hunger, death and disease were rife in the ghettoes, and German authorities were instructed to shoot anyone who ventured beyond the ghetto's perimeter.

The Warsaw ghetto was one of the largest, housing 490,000 people during its 30-month existence; an existence that only began its end when 265,000 inhabitants were taken to meet their death at the Treblinka death camp. Amidst this horrific situation Courpasson and Marti testify to how despite the extremity of the oppression productive resistance was both present and effective. Of course this resistance did not overthrow the oppressor, but it was a situation where 'oppressed people transcend [...] complicity and subtle forms of silent subversions while still maintaining the advantages of secrecy to act against the dominant order that shapes their everyday life' (p. 865). This operated through a 'collective ethics of resistance' (p. 865) where people engaged in meaningful and productive social relation to enable survival. In the Warsaw Ghetto, this was enacted through the creation of an underground society that revitalized the forms of social interaction and relations that the Nazis had intended to eliminate through the very process of ghettoization. The result was an 'underlife' in the ghetto involving the provision of food beyond the meagre rations provided by the Nazis, the organization of cultural activities, creation of schools and libraries, the formation of illegal political parties, and the creation of underground newspapers. It also involved the creation of a secret archive designed to ensure that the catastrophic tragedy afflicted on Warsaw's Jews would not be forgotten by future generations.

As Courpasson and Marti (2018) put it: 'the deeds of the ghetto's inhabitants demonstrate a practical work of ethics accomplished through resistance, oriented to freedom-seeking initiatives of individuals embedded in powerless situations' (p. 866). This ethically motivated resistance sought to enable both human dignity and survival, against all odds. The second example is more contemporary and comes from Vachhani and Pullen's study of the Everyday Sexism Project (ESP); an online social movement based on a website that allows users to share experiences of sexism and inequality. The purpose of the ESP is to 'amplify everyday experiences and to empower women to act against sexism' (p. 27) in a safe and non-judgemental space. Founded in 2012 by Laura Bates, some 18 months later 50,000 women have posted stories. Sheena Vachhani and Alison Pullen conceptualize the practices of the ESP as a form of 'infrapolitical' resistance to sexism born specifically out of a feminist ethico-politics. Such infrapolitics 'emerges at grassroots level and between individuals in the form of affective solidarity, which become necessary in challenging neoliberal threats to women's opportunity and equality' (p. 23). Through raising awareness and creating solidarity, the ESP proved to be an effective form of organizing that resisted sexism by calling 'for a cultural and social shift in attitudes to women and violence against women' (p. 28). This call gained global political significance as Bates used the ESP as the basis of public talks and interviews, as well as gaining international political and media attention through presenting to the United Nations Commission on the Status of Women and the publication of the book *Everyday Sexism* (Bates, 2014).

The ESP enabled individual, yet shared, experiences of sexism suffered by women to become not only achieved but also collectively mobilized. This is a direct enactment of a corporeal ethics in that it showed how 'feminist resistance develops based on an embodied response to injustice [...] and affective solidarity, which [...] mobilises experience and empathy in the struggle' (p. 29). A key dimension of this is resistance to sexism at work, with the ESP testifying to the existence of this sexism as well as challenging its institutionalization in organizations. Its political purchase is that of 'cultivating social sensitivity is a way of becoming attuned to injustice, and [enabling] the injustices created by sexism or racism, privilege and oppression to be addressed' (p. 42).

Corporeal ethics/political resistance

The two examples that we have just considered, while vastly different in many ways, demonstrate the very real possibilities for how a corporeal ethics based on a care for other people and a shared direction can lead to potent forms of resistance against even the most extreme and entrenched forms of oppression. This is an ethico-politics arising from corporeal generosity, and that, while being organized, rests initially in an embodied and affective concern and care for other people. This organizing is very different from the coordination of contemporary capitalism through systems of contract, exchange, and reciprocity (Diprose, 2002: 10) and economies of calculated self-advantage (Jones, 2003). The rational pursuit of self-interest dominates the Western imaginary in its reach and power, and it is this as well that needs to be resisted. Indeed, it is seen as quite 'normal' that 'social relations are subject to calculation and expectation of return in terms of values that favour the bodies that already dominate the sociopolitical sphere' (Diprose, 2002: 171); that is, by and large, able-bodied, heterosexual, white, male, well-manicured, and well-dressed bodies. For us, it is a critique of the practical conditions of such social relations that can offer an ethical basis on which such resistance can be founded. This is an ethics of radical alterity and radical generosity.

It is its origin in the pre-reflective that marks generosity's corporeality; its affective operation spontaneously originating through the body before reflection and before ego. Such generosity 'eschews the calculation characteristic of an economy of exchange' (Diprose, 2002: 5); the very forms of reciprocity that reduce corporate ethics to a mode of patriarchal self-interested instrumentality (Rhodes and Westwood, 2016). Corporeal ethics does not provide any 'groundwork for an ethics of organisation' (Hancock, 2008: 1371), instead working to destabilize any such ground through acts of ethico-political resistance. Even though there can be no 'particular program of political practice that could better regulate unconditional generosity' (Diprose, 2002: 186) corporeal ethics takes practical forms when it mobilizes organized political action that results 'those discourses that totalise and normalise bodies, that hide their own morality [...] behind claims to objectivity and detachment' (p. 194). Such an ethics is an ongoing struggle rather than a utopian destination. Therefore, it is always an:

unfinished project, [that] can be observed in our embodied experience of open relations with others in organisations in response to a rational managerial enclosure of difference [...] ethico-political dynamics in contemporary actions of resistance [are] a form of non-managerial difference that challenges the status quo of managerial control, which imposes an ethics of compliance.

(Alakavulkar and Alamgir, 2018: 39)

Corporeal ethics offers the possibility for an ethical appreciation of resistance to oppressive organizations and institutions in a way that respects and preserves difference. This politics of radical difference is especially relevant to organizations given the 'increasingly powerful individualising and normalising processes shaping the life worlds of worker-citizens in a globalising risk society' (Kelly et al., 2007: 267) as well as 'the massive inequalities of status and power that corporations routinely create and reproduce' (Parker, 2003: 195; see also Barkan, 2013). This attests to a long-established political tradition that seeks to achieve social justice through the removal of discrimination and the celebration of difference by placing intercorporeal generosity centre stage. Corporeal ethics prompts an invitation for people in organizations to be open to, and moved by, intercorporeal relations with others. Nevertheless, there are no guarantees, only possibilities whose outcomes cannot be pre-determined; ethics is something that we can do, but not something that ever gets finally done.

Dominant approaches to the study of ethics and organizations have sought to pursue ethicality within the bounds of that which can be organized and managed; it has been largely informed by 'a managerial agenda and an ethics of compliance' (Alakavuklar and Alamgir, 2018: 39). These approaches put the responsibility for ethics solely in the hands of those who are charged with the task of organizing and in so doing fail to 'challenge the dominant assumptions that shape not only organizational relations but also the social and economic relations that create injustice' and fail to account for 'the ethico-political base of resistance' (p. 40).

In contrast to this, corporeal ethics is diffuse; it is embedded throughout organizations as well as outside of them. Corporeal ethics can lead to individual and collective ethical action that is neither controlled nor circumscribed by authority. In the form of resistance, corporeal ethics in organizations emerges when power is put at the mercy of ethics, acknowledging too that 'ethics is far too important to be left in the hands of business' (Rhodes, 2014: 735). Ethics, understood as originating in corporeal generosity and the pre-reflexive exposure to the other, is that which provides the foundation for and justification of political action; action realized through the exercise of resistance. Moreover, the openness of corporeal generosity demands that ethics is always an unfinished project that cannot rely upon or be firmly lodged within administrative arrangements. That is not to say that corporeal ethics cannot be present in organizations, of course, it can, most especially through the bodies of people striving towards an openness to the other that does not seek final refuge in managerially imposed organizational schemes, be they exploitative or well meaning.

Corporeal ethics does not offer the false promise of a righteousness that might finally be achieved to render organizations' morally impeccable status. Indeed, corporeal ethics is not the idea that supports the idea that such 'achievement' is possible. More modestly, we have highlighted a different location where ethically informed practice might be found as it arises from corporeal ethics. Clearly much goes on in the name of ethically informed resistance to organizations, be it in the form, inter alia, of resisting gendered and racial discrimination, resisting exploitative organizational practice, and resisting managerial bullying. It is with such acts that a corporeal ethics of organizations might be located. Questioning and supplementing the rational and managerial approach that characterizes much of the research in organizational ethics, corporeal ethics is pre-reflective in origin, embodied in character and political in practice. In this frame, ethics in organization manifests politically through resistance that seeks to defy categorization and normalization and the forms of discrimination they invoke. This is a resistance borne out of affective and corporeal encounters with others; encounters marked by generosity and welcome. Corporeal ethics informs an ethico-politics, that is a 'politics of generosity [that] begins with all of us, it begins and remains in trouble, and it begins with the act' (Diprose, 2002: 188), a 'passionate politics that would work through generosity for a justice that is yet to arrive' (p. 194). This is a project of ethico-political resistance and critique that works against forms of coercion, inequity, and discrimination that organizations so frequently and easily reproduce

Care needs to be taken to acknowledge that an embodied ethics is not one that demands a priori agreement ahead of the ethical encounter or experience being entered into; that is precisely the rational, normative and totalizing ethical tendency that an embodied approach can contest and counter. Would ethics exist if we all agreed precisely on what it was and how it might be achieved? We think not, given the radical particularity of the embodied experience that might demand ethical engagement or response. Against the possibility of a powerful socially imposed ethical false consensus, we retain the hope that through our interaction with each other and with the world, we might foster ways of organizational life that resist domination and oppression in favour of the enactment of care and respect for difference as it is lived and experienced.

References

Ackroyd, S., and Thompson, P. (1999) *Organizational Misbehaviour*. London: Sage.

Alakavuklar, O.N., and Alamgir, F. (2018) Ethics of resistance in organisations: A conceptual proposal. *Journal of Business Ethics*, 149(1): 31–43.

Alcadipani, R., Hassard, J., and Islam, G. (2018) 'I Shot the Sheriff': Irony, sarcasm and the changing nature of workplace resistance. *Journal of Management Studies*, 55(8): 1452–1487.

Amis, J.M., Mair, J., and Munir, K. (2019) The organizational reproduction of inequality. *Academy of Management Annals*, published online ahead of print: https://doi.org/10.5465/annals.2017.0033

Ball, K. (2005) Organization, surveillance and the body: Towards a politics of resistance. *Organization*, 12(1): 89–108.

Barkan, J. (2013) *Corporate Sovereignty: Law and Government under Capitalism*. Minneapolis: University of Minnesota Press.

Bates, L. (2014) *Everyday Sexism*. London: Simon and Schuster.

Bell, E., Meriläinen, S., Taylor, S., and Tienari, J. (2019) Time's up! Feminist theory and activism meets organization studies. *Human Relations*, 72(1): 4–22.

Bevir, M. (1999) Foucault, power and institutions. *Political Studies*, XLVII: 345–359.

Burawoy, M. (1979) *Manufacturing Consent: Change in the Labor Process under Monopoly Capitalism*. Chicago, IL: University of Chicago Press.

Burrell, G. (1992) The organization of pleasure. In H. Willmott and M. Alvesson (Eds.), pp. 165–183, *Critical Management Studies*. London: Sage.

Collinson, D. (1994) Strategies of resistance: Power, knowledge and resistance in the workplace. In J.M. Jermier, D. Knights, and W.R. Nord (Eds.), pp. 25–68, *Resistance and Power in Organisations*. London: Routledge.

Collinson, D. (2002) Managing humour. *Journal of Management Studies*, 39: 269–288.

Collinson, D. (2005) Discussion of Thomas and Davies: Refuting romanticism: The value of feminist perspectives for understanding resistance. *Organization*, 12(5): 741–746.

Courpasson, D., and Marti, I. (2019) Collective ethics of resistance: The organization of survival in the Warsaw Ghetto. *Organisation*, online ahead of print: https://doi.org/10.1177/1350508418820993

Critchley, S. (2008) *Infinitely Demanding: Ethics of Commitment, Politics of Resistance*. London: Verso.

De Coster, M. (2020) Towards a relational ethics in pandemic times and beyond: Limited accountability, collective performativity and new subjectivity. *Gender, Work and Organization*, 27(5): 747–753.

Diprose, R. (2002) *Corporeal Generosity: On Giving with Nietzsche, Merleau-Ponty and Levinas (SUNY Series in Gender Theory)*. New York: State University of New York Press.

Fleming, P. (2005) Metaphors of resistance. *Management Communication Quarterly*, 19(1): 45–66.

Fleming, P. (2007) Sexuality, power and resistance in the workplace. *Organization Studies* 28(2): 239–256.

Fleming, P., and Sewell, G. (2002) Looking for the good soldier, Svejk: Alternative modalities of resistance in the contemporary workplace. *Sociology*, 36(4): 857–873.

Fleming, P., and Spicer, A. (2003) Working at a cynical distance: Implications for power, surveillance and resistance. *Organisation*, 10: 157–179.

Foster, W.M., and Wiebe, E. (2010) Praxis makes perfect: Recovering the ethical promise of critical management studies. *Journal of Business Ethics*, 94(2): 271–283.

Fotaki, M., Metcalfe, B.D., and Harding, N. (2014) Writing materiality into management and organisation studies through and with Luce Irigaray. *Human Relations*, 67(10): 1239–1263.

Hancock, P. (2008) Embodied generosity and an ethics of organization. *Organization Studies*, 29(10): 1357–1373.

Holvino, E. (2010) Intersections: The simultaneity of race, gender and class in organization studies. *Gender, Work and Organisation*, 17(3): 248–277.

Iedema, R., and Rhodes, C. (2010) The undecided space of ethics in organizational surveillance. *Organization Studies*, 31(2): 199–217.

Iedema, R., Rhodes, C., and Scheeres, H. (2006) Surveillance, resistance, observance: Exploring the teleoaffective intensity of identity (at) work. *Organization Studies*, 17(8): 1111–1130.

Jermier, J.M., Knights, D., and Nord, W.R. (Eds.) (1994) *Resistance and Power in Organisations.* London: Routledge.

Jones, C. (2003) As if business ethics were possible, 'within such limits' .... *Organization,* 10(2): 223–248.

Kelly, P., Allender, S., and Colquhoun, D. (2007) New work ethics? The corporate athlete's back end index and organisational performance. *Organisation,* 14(2): 267–285.

Knights, D., and McCabe, D. (2000) 'Ain't misbehavin'? Opportunities for resistance under new forms of quality management. *Sociology,* 34(3): 421–436.

Knights, D., and Vurdubakis, T. (1994) Foucault, power, resistance and all that. In J.M. Jermier, D. Knights, and W.R. Nord (Eds.), pp. 167–198, *Resistance and Power in Organisations.* London: Routledge.

McCabe, D., Ciuk, S., and Gilbert, M. (2020) 'There is a crack in everything': An ethnographic study of pragmatic resistance in a manufacturing organization. *Human Relations,* 73(7): 953–980.

McEwen, C., Pullen, A., and Rhodes, C. (2021) Sexual harassment at work: A leadership problem. *RAE-Revista de Administração de Empresas (Journal of Business Management),* 61(2): 1–7.

McMurray, R., Pullen, A., and Rhodes, C. (2011) Ethical subjectivity and politics in organisations: A case of health care tendering. *Organization,* 18(4): 541–561.

Montes, V., and Pombo, M.D.P. (2019) Ethics of care, emotional work, and collective action of solidarity: The Patronas in Mexico. *Gender, Place & Culture,* 26(4): 559–580.

Mumby, D. (2005) Theorizing resistance in organisations: A dialectic approach. *Management Communication Quarterly,* 19(1): 19–44.

Mumby, D. (2008) Theorising the future of critical organizational studies. In H. Hansen and D. Barry (Eds.), pp. 27–28, *The Sage Handbook of New Approaches to Management and Organization.* London: Sage.

Mumby, D.K., Thomas, R, Martí, I., and Seidl, D. (2017) Resistance redux. *Organisation Studies,* 38(9): 1157–1183.

Nentwich, J., and Hoyer, P. (2012) Part-time work as practising resistance: The power of counter-arguments. *British Journal of Management,* 24(4): 557–570.

Parker, M. (1999) Capitalism, subjectivity and ethics: Debating labour process analysis. *Organization Studies,* 20(1): 25–45.

Parker, M. (2003) Ethics, politics and organising. *Organization,* 10(2): 187–203.

Pullen, A., Rhodes, C., McEwen, C., and Liu, H. (2019) Radical politics, intersectionality and leadership for diversity in organizations. *Management Decision.* https://doi.org/10.1108/MD-02-2019-0287

Raffnsøe, S., Mennicken, A., and Miller, P. (2019) The Foucault effect in organization studies. *Organization Studies,* 40(2): 155–182.

Rhodes, C. (2009) All I want to do is get that check and get drunk. *Journal of Organizational Change Management,* 22(4): 396–401.

Rhodes, C. (2014) Ethical anarchism, business ethics and the politics of disturbance. *Ephemera: Theory and Politics in Organization,* 14(4): 725–737.

Rhodes, C. (2016) Democratic business ethics: Volkswagen's emissions scandal and the disruption of corporate sovereignty. *Organisation Studies*, 37(10): 1501–1518.

Rhodes, C., and Pullen, A. (2018) Critical business ethics: From corporate self-interest to the glorification of the sovereign pater. *International Journal of Management Reviews*, 20(2): 483–499.

Rhodes, C., and Westwood, R. (2016) The limits of generosity: Lessons on ethics, economy, and reciprocity in Kafka's the metamorphosis. *Journal of Business Ethics*, 133(2): 235–248.

Spicer, A., and Böhm, S. (2007) Moving management: Theorizing struggles against the hegemony of management. *Organization Studies*, 28(11): 1667–1698.

Thomas, R., and Davies, A. (2005) What have the feminists done for us? Feminist theory and organizational resistance. *Organization*, 12(5): 711–740.

Thompson, P. (1989) *The Nature of Work: An Introduction to Debates on the Labour Process*, 2nd ed. Houndmills: MacMillan.

Thompson, P., and Ackroyd, S. (1995) All quiet on the workplace front? A critique of recent trends in British industrial sociology. *Sociology*, 29(4): 615–633.

Townley, B. (2005) Controlling Foucault. *Organization*, 12(5): 643–648.

Vachhani, S.J. (2020) Envisioning a democratic culture of difference: Feminist ethics and the politics of dissent in social movements. *Journal of Business Ethics*, 164(4): 745–757.

Vachhani, S.J., and Pullen, A. (2019) Ethics, politics and feminist organizing: Writing feminist infrapolitics and affective solidarity into everyday sexism. *Human Relations*, 72(1): 23–47.

Westwood, R., and Johnston, A. (2012) Reclaiming authentic selves: Control, resistive humour and identity work in the office. *Organization Studies*, 9(6): 787–808.

Ybema, S., Thomas, R., and Hardy, C. (2016) Organizational change and resistance: An identity perspective. In D. Courpasson and S. Vallas (Eds.), pp. 386–404, *The SAGE Handbook of Resistance*. London: Sage.

Younes, D., Courpasson, D., and Jacob, M.R. (2020) Ethics from below: Secrecy and the maintenance of ethics. *Journal of Business Ethics*, 163(3): 451–466.

Zanin, A.C., and Bisel, R.S. (2020) Concertive resistance: How overlapping team identifications enable collective organisational resistance. *Culture and Organization*, 26(3): 231–249.

Ziarek, E. (2001) *An Ethics of Dissensus: Postmodernity, Feminism, and the Politics of Radical Democracy*. Stanford, CA: Stanford University Press.

5   The affective organization of corporeal ethics

Iris Marian Young's (2005) foundational essay *Throwing Like a Girl* reminds us that our lived bodies cannot escape the 'facticity' of their materiality. These are also bodies that can be subject to discrimination and harassment in particular environments; organizations being a case in point. The individual body – sexed, sexual, raced, gendered, and abled – is, as we have been attesting in this book, also the place from which corporeal ethics emerges. This is 'a physical body acting and experiencing in a specific sociocultural context; it is body-in-situation' (Young, 2005: 16). For Young '[t]he lived body is particular in its morphology, material similarities, and differences from other bodies' (p. 25): it is both the same as other bodies and unique unto itself. While fuelled by desire and affect, bodies are also social. They are understood in relation to the structures and power relations they find themselves in, and the opportunities and resources available to them. As part of this, ours are 'habituated bodies reacting to, and reproducing, and modifying structures' (ibid: 26).

Bodies are both material and discursive, and the freedoms attributed to bodies are constrained by the social structures that surround them. Inequality and discrimination are central to those constraints, with some bodies more able to do things than others. We are living in times where inequalities are increasingly at stake in the world; inequalities that are unfairly experienced by certain typed bodies. This is not only income and wealth inequality but also relates to access to health, rights to bodily autonomy, subjection to police brutality, and living in war and political conflict. Since 2020, COVID-19 has highlighted, if not exacerbated, such inequalities and discrimination as inherent in the global economic system. This is a system where poverty, lack of health care, unaffordable housing, and climate catastrophe are central features (Fraser et al., 2019).

DOI: 10.4324/9781003031048-5

In this final chapter, we close our discussion of corporeal ethics and the relations between situated bodies by attending specifically to how this ethics, while arising in each body, gains effect when it is mobilized collectively as a response to the injustice of inequality. While earlier chapters have focused on ethics in the context of formal organizations, here we move to a discussion of the organization of ethics in the context of political action more broadly. Our concern is how corporeal ethics moves to change the world in the name of justice and equality through the assembly of bodies in communal political action. With this we see how the ethico-politics of resistance that we considered in Chapter 4 is itself something that can be collectively organized through affective relations. This resistance is still, however, part of an organizational ethics, in that it is commonly directed at power that is exercised from the seat of formal or bureaucratic authority, whether that seat is in Wall Street (for the Occupy movement), in the Santa Monica headquarters of Miramax where Harvey Weinstein worked (for the #MeToo movement) or in the bureaucracy of the police force (in the case of Black Lives Matter movement).

Focusing on collective social action against the exercise and abuse of formal authority extends beyond what bodies can do individually or in relation with other bodies. Every individual atomized body is limited through its inherent reliance on others for survival such that it is only collectively that we can endure as well as overcome the limits of the sole and vulnerable body. We thus turn to the ethico-political possibilities of communal intercorporeality and what that means for an ethics of collective organizing and resistance. With such collectively our attention also moves from ethics to justice, as affective sensibilities, material resources, and care for one another need to be distributed among the multitude of bodies, each and every one deserving of care.

Corporeal ethics manifests in the world across the mobilization of diverse bodies that are both unified and different. Such an ethics is about caring for others who are both known and unknown, but with whom one shares some level of communal identification if not through humanity alone. This ethical mobilization of bodies is not necessarily about physical movement. Corporeal ethics becomes social with the ethical desire to join together, whether it be in resistance against oppressive forces, or in solidarity towards social justice. This collective organization of bodies can stand against dominant power regimes which benefit from the differentiation of social groups and individuals from others. In our time, we see this in movements that seek to counter the injustices resulting from neoliberalism, colonialism, and patriarchy as they are sustained by sexed, class raced, political separation, and enslavement.

Our contention is that collective bodies ethically motivated to social justice threaten the social and organizational structures that reinforce oppressive power relations between the more powerful and the less powerful, and between those who enjoy safety security and those who are thrust into precariousness. This was evident when people communed in public space in the Occupy Movement in 2011 and 2012 to protest gross economic inequalities. It was evident too as women, and some men, took to the streets together in 2018 under the banner of the #MeToo movement to say no to sexual harassment. Collective demands for justice do not end with a utopian resolution to all of society's ills. Justice is an ongoing pursuit that requires persistent vigilance. Today we are witnessing widespread and acrimonious attacks against people on the basis of how they identify. In Hungary we have seen the removal of LGBTIQA+ curriculum. In Poland abortions have been made illegal. In the United States, Australia and elsewhere politicians have sought to remove critical race theory (CRT) from the school curriculum. While each of these examples are forms of local oppression, they also show that without global resistance and solidarity, regressive and damaging political positions can gain hold, with people suffering real consequences including bodily harm as a result.

Bodies are shaped by geopolitics, and it is the location of geopolitics that ethico-politics becomes viable through the mobilization of bodies in their diversity. We are mindful that different people do not necessarily share common oppressions (hooks, 1981), and on that basis are concerned with the ethico-politics that are possible both within and across these differences through communal organizing. This evokes a demand for democracy, for a collectively organization committed to equality and participation over domination at atomization. It is through the collective that we can live what Young calls 'vibrant democratic life' (Young, 1990) where we can resist the tendency for difference to lead to discrimination, oppression, marginalization, and inequality. Arising initially in the affective desire to care for others, corporeal ethics is not just the matter of one's self or one's relationship with particular other people. More broadly it is the manifestation of that desire to care in a broader political practice of democratic political action in the name of justice and equality.

An ethics of recognition: towards the collective

As Judith Butler (2005) argues, ethics is wrapped up in the ability of one to give an account of oneself in pursuit of the 'desire for recognition of oneself as a viable subject' (Tyler, 2020: 11). Butler is concerned with the idea of individual performativity and its relation to ethical responsibility and being 'held to account' by and for others. To give such an account is not for one's own benefit, but rather pleads with the other for acknowledgement and recognition. In this accounting for oneself, one is called to provide a 'convincing ethical defence of one's claim for recognition, particularly when that claim involves accounting for one's difference' (ibid.: 11). This ethical defence is a political process of opening oneself to others scrutiny in a desire of recognition. Responsibility is vulnerability, in that it requires the self to be subject to the demands of the other. But recognition is not granted equally, with injustice arising from this maldistribution of recognition. Not all self accounts are equal, and the issue Butler takes up is 'how power operates to regulate and determine who counts as human, to shape and condition the scene of recognition, and to circumscribe the types of ethical encounter that might take place there' (Lloyd, 2015: 167).

This focus on the self as a performative site for ethical subjectivity reflects on what different bodies can do – and undo – together. Drawing on Butler's ideas to think about collective recognition is fruitful. As we see today, ongoing claims for recognition for people is evident across the globe, from the subjection of the Uyghurs in China, to Indigenous recognition as the First Peoples of what we now call Australia. These collective calls for recognition reveal both the 'ethical defence' and the political intent of the collective. Following Butler this is ethical when attention turns from the self to the other. To simply ask 'the personal question, what makes my own life bearable' is important in its drive for self-preservation. With ethics, however, we must ask 'from a position of power, and from the point of view of distributive justice, what makes, or ought to make, the lives of others bearable?' The quality of one's response to that question, for Butler, demonstrates a normative ethical commitment to how one lives one's life, and, crucially, reflects 'what constitutes the human, the distinctively human life, and what does not' (Butler, 2004a: 17).

Humanity, following Butler, is not intrinsic to the possession of a human body, but emerges from a sense of collectivity and care for others. To give an account of oneself is not just about the self, but is based on a 'non-violent ethics of reflexive reciprocity' that accepts our inherent interdependence and the realization that 'we are, from the start, ethically implicated in the lives of others' (Butler 2005: 64). Butler highlights how the relational character of our selves is what ethics and politics are formed from. Relationality is about our ethical difference and ethical connectedness as people, and it is the 'means by which we are both dispossessed and constituted within the sphere of recognition' (Tyler, 2020: 119). Ethical relationality is premised upon recognition of the other as other; it fundamental to not only the performativity of subjectivity but also the very possibility of a collective ethics. This is a 'plural performativity' (Butler and Athanasiou, 2013: 157; 151) that is developed based on an ethics of corporeal vulnerability. This is not an idealized citizen but the body of a real person in political connection with others that relate in a manner that exceeds the limitations of 'neoliberal regimes of economization of life?' (Butler and Athanasiou, 2013: 176). Ethical intercorporeality is not about reciprocal exchange motivated by the maximization of self-interest. It is about being open and responsive to the needs and struggles of other people, and for the benefit of all.

Standing together: the ethical and political imperative of assembly

Throughout history the appearance of people's bodies in an organized way for recognition and protest is evident. This includes activist strategies such as street marches, public resistance performances, boycotts, and sit-ins. In recent times, we have witnessed intense organizing to resist populism, racism, sexism, corruption, climate change, and genocide. Most recently social movements and organized protests have taken to the streets, such as Extinction Rebellion, Black Lives Matter, Women's Marches, LGBTIQ+, pro-Trans, and anti-femicide protests. The mobilization and assembly of bodies is central to social activism through a proliferation of bodies across difference that stands against violence and injustice. These are bodies that move together towards recognition and rights. To what extent, however, can such political action be seen to be connected to a corporeal ethics of recognition? The bodily collectivity of the assembly is not an adequate answer. Indeed, assembly can be used across the political sphere for emancipatory and non-emancipatory purposes. Groups such as those upholding populist or even fascist politics, white supremacy, gun rights, and anti-vaccinations organize, gather, and protest in a similar manner.

What differentiates collective mobilizing as political action based on corporeal ethics is a desire to redress discrimination, loss, inequality vulnerability, precarity, and injustice, and in the name of creating liveable lives for others. There is however, no ethical purity in politics and the reality remains that what constitutes justice is always contestable. Protest movements are not without critique, as different bodies come under attack for being exclusionary. For example, the Australian Women's Marches against sexual violence and lack of government action came under attack for their own identity politics. United, these marches garnered unprecedented support and recognition for women's lives and rights. However, they were also criticized on the basis of being blind to class and racial differences, and the broader forms of oppression faced by working class women and women of colour. Further, the ability to gather in protest is itself a position with collective political expression not being available for all. In Recep Tayyip Erdogan's Turkey LGBT protestors are arrested and vilified. In Rio de Janeiro, Mariella Franco was shot while speaking against police brutality.

The right to assemble and to join with others in a common call for justice is itself a precursor to the possibility of collective ethical resistance. Assembled bodies are the site of collective corporeal ethics, perpetuated by political autonomy, grounded in situatedness, enacting an ethical sensibility between bodies in relation. For Butler (2015) assemblies are 'recognition-based bodily presence' (p. 169). Butler argues for the political power of co-presence where 'showing up, standing, breathing, moving, standing still, speech, and silence are all [...] an unforeseen form of political performativity' (p. 18). Moreover the act of assembly is as a mode of organizing that not only exercises a 'a plural and performative right to appear' but also represents 'a bodily demand [...] for a more liveable set economic, social and political conditions no longer afflicted by induced forms of precarity' (Tyler, 2020: 11).

In thinking through a collective corporeal ethics, political assembly represents the ethical and political imperative at the heart of a collective demand for recognition. Assembly thus moves from an individual desire for recognition, to one that becomes collective and focuses on the recognition of, and care for, others as is only possible through a larger collective struggle. For the marginalized and minoritized, the abject and erased, this collective demand becomes central to living a liveable life. Collective struggle operates beyond ego-centric self-satisfaction in the hope that collective recognition of the many can be gained against economic and political injustices. As Butler describes:

> Only when bodies assemble on the street, in the square, or in other forms of public space (including virtual ones) they are exercising a plural and performative right to appear, one that asserts and instates the body during the political field, and which, in its expressive and signifying function, delivers a bodily demand for a more liveable set of economic, social, and political conditions no longer afflicted by induced forms of precarity.
>
> (Butler, 2015: 11)

The simple act of bodies being together, for Butler, 'enacts a provisional and plural form of co-existence that constitutes a distinct ethical and social alternative to "responsibilization"' (ibid.: 16). The responsibilization to which Butler refers is that which comes from a neoliberal ideological insistence on the primacy of individual over collective responsibility, whose privileging self-reliance is that harbinger of social isolation. The assembly eschewing such isolation through the embodied performance of collective responsibility. Embodied protest as a form of political action and women's roles in mobilizing collective protests are well documented. As Marianna Fotaki and Maria Daskalaki (2020) note, 'women use diverse means to promote the politics of visibility, erasing public and private distinctions as they defend their communities' right to live in unpolluted environments' (p. 1). The assembly of human bodies, and the relation between those bodies, is a means through which an ethically motivated democratic politics can be mobilized. This is a democracy where oppression of particular 'types' of bodies and their continued capacity for existence is pursued by real people working together in proximity.

Demonstrations against precarity, such as we have seen with the Colombian mass protests Cali Nationale Resistance in 2021, are political moments that make visible democracy. This is an 'ethical obligation that is grounded in precarity' (Butler, 2005: 119). Further, this 'shared condition of precarity situates our political lives, even as precarity is differentially distributed' (p. 96). Moreover, such forms of assembly are democratic in that they demand recognition of the *demos* – the people – whose plight might otherwise be ignored and 'slipped quietly into the shadows of public life' (Butler in Butler and Athanasiou, 2013: 151). Assembly is an act of collective and embodied ethico-politics:

> The collective assembling of bodies is an exercise of the popular will, and a way of asserting, in bodily form, one of the most basic presuppositions of democracy, namely that political and public institutions are bound to represent the people, and to do so in ways that establish equality as a presupposition of social and political existence. So when those institutions become structured in such a way that certain populations become disposable, are interpolated as disposable, become deprived on a future, of education, of stable and fulfilling work, then surely the assemblies fulfil another function, not only the expression of justifiable rage, but their assertion of their very social organization on principles of equality.
> (Butler in Butler and Athanasiou, 2013: 151–152)

That such a democratic privileging of equality is ethics, its ethics is not about a desire to pursue one's own rights as an atomized individual, it is an ethics that seeks equality for the collective; a situation where 'the "I" becomes undone by its ethical relation to the "you"' (Butler, 2015: 110). Butler underlines how, such ethical relations originate through the self's vulnerability to the demands of others, such that our very existence as 'selves' is always already defined through our ethical relations with other people. Ethics engages us in relations with the other who we do not know, the stranger, alerting us to the existential fact that we live amidst a world of difference. This demands an ethics where '[b]eing at ease with strangeness; knowing that we have no choice but to live with difference, whatever differences come to matter in specific times and places' (The Care Collective, 2020: 95). Assembly enables this coming together in community – across difference – in strangeness, for democracy, equality, and justice.

Social justice: a radical democratic project

The vulnerability to the other that permeates corporeal ethics when manifesting collectively in assembly is an ethical demand for justice and for the recognition of difference. It is on this basis that we can assert the entanglement of corporeal ethics with a project of radical democracy. In this regard we need to distinguish between a gathering of bodies that constitutes a 'riot' and one that constitute an 'assembly'; the former being riotous and violent, and the latter being a form of collectivity and deliberation. As Butler describes, while

> we continue to need assemblies to realize democracies. We have to be able to distinguish between assemblies that are self-reflective and are inclusive – seeking to exemplify modes of democratic participation and debate – and those who are giving up on democracy.
> (Butler, 2016: n.p.)

The rights of gender equality serve as a valuable example of the relation between corporeal ethics and democracy, in particular radical democracy. Butler (2005) writes that for this social justice struggle 'to be characterized as a radical democratic project, it is necessary to realize that we are but one population who has been and can be exposed to conditions of precarity and disenfranchisement' (p. 66). Identifying as a woman, for example, may be a position from which to assert one's rights based on a history of disenfranchisement, but it is not the only position from which to make that assertion. Democratic struggles are plural,

Butler insists, such that 'the rights to gender' while identifiable as a social movement, is one that relies on the relations between people rather than the assertion of individualism. Interdependencies and alliances between different gender identifications, as well as other forms of difference, stand against a neoliberal privileging of individualism and its attendant idea that identity is a form of personal possession rather than being the location of relations of sameness and difference with others. Interdependency is the condition of democracy such that the struggle for democratic justice is a 'struggle for an egalitarian social and political order which a liveable interdependency becomes' (p. 69).

This notion of radical democracy is not to be equated with the formal institutions and practices of liberal democracy, most especially when the latter becomes entwined with elite corporate power (Rhodes et al., 2020). Moreover,

> radical democracy differs from liberal democratic government in that it retains the root meaning of democracy as being that the power to rule must be retained with the social body; with the people rather than with a political class or the institutions of the state.
> (Rhodes, 2016: 1510)

The political assembly of bodies is a paradigm example of this radical democracy. Assembly exemplifies how:

> radical democracy bears witness to marginalized voices excluded from the prevailing status quo and enacts a particular ethics rested in the radical questioning and subversion of the totalizing tendencies of power [...] With radical democracy, the political task is to fight against the powers, injustices and inequalities that affect people not just politically, but also materially [...and...] directed towards a liveable and sustainable future.
> (Rhodes et al., 2020: 628)

Radical democracy is informed by a primary respect for difference and equality as exercised through 'dissensus' rather than a powerfully imposed false 'consensus'. It involves a non-violent confirmation of difference in the name of all of the people (Mouffe 1996: 2000). Following Chantal Mouffe, with radical democracy, public life, and its physical spaces, are the sites where difference should engage in productive conflict without the assumption of an idealistic or utopian realization of the needs of all (Thomassen, 2010). Instead it is the pursuit of justice and equality, not the pretence of its achievement, that marks out the democratic project. It is an ethically disciplined 'challenge to the dominant apparatus of power' (Munro, 2014: 1129) through an assertion of 'political agency on behalf of and for the people' (Robbins, 2011: 62). Collective corporeal ethics through assembly can be understood as a practice of radical democracy. For such an ethics, Sheena Vachhani (2020) highlights the need to 're-imagine the constitutive exclusions faced by marginalized or vulnerable groups' (2020: 755), recognizing that we live in social systems while desiring new ones. Vachhani proposed an ethics of dissensus where power and political difference can be confronted without assuming that entrenched differences based on race gender, class or sexuality can be overcome once and for all, but rather that effective democratic politics lies in the ongoing confrontation of those differences in the name of justice. That this is done without violence is a sign of the quality of democracy, and the ethical vulnerability to difference. It is only with such vulnerability that bodies come together, and that society changes in the direction of equality and justice. Corporeal ethics manifests as assembly. For Vachhani this surfaces political action and activism is reliant on the entwinement of bodies, practices, and ethics that enable affectual relationships, organizing, and resistance.

Vachhani follows Ewa Płonowska Ziarek (2001) in attesting to an ethics of dissensus located in radical democracy. This emphasizes a concern with 'the role of ethical respect for the Other in proliferating democratic struggle against racial, sexist and class oppression' (Ziarek, 2001: 9). It is worth emphasizing here the relationship between 'struggle' and 'democracy'. Democracy is not a finite state which one achieves by having the right institutions in place; it is an ongoing practice in the name justice and equality, whose pursuit does not cease. Struggle is a persistent feature of democracy, not one that results in an end state where difference dissolves into a consensual utopia. Such is the 'constitutive antagonism of democracy' (Ziarek, 2001: 9). Vachhani (2020) shows how such antagonism and dissent are constitutive of social movements premised on ethical relations. Exemplified in feminist movements, this illustrates

> the complex dynamics of dissent and radical democracy based on intercorporeal and embodied differences' and how this can 'challenge systems of oppression and the constitutive exclusions faced by different women with the promise of hope and vulnerability of the embodied and generous ethical relation.
>
> (p. 755)

For Vachhani, the collective acts of political movements are part of a corporeal ethico-political practice that challenges systems of difference that produce and reproduce oppression.

While Vachhani's discussion focuses on feminism and activist politics, we can draw parallels with Angela Davis' (2016) discussion of struggle and intersectionality as a more general mode of striving for human liberation. Like Butler, Davis positions politics in opposition to the individualism that has become entrenched by neoliberalism. Davis asserts that 'progressive struggles – whether they are focussed on racism, repression, poverty or other issues – are doomed to fail if they do not also attempt to develop a consciousness of the insidious promotion of capitalist individualism' (p. 1). Collective struggle, for Davis, requires solidarity and mutuality as part of a democratic practice that is not located in the heights of elected power, but in the power of grassroots movements. By way of example:

> Movements, feminist movements, other movements, are most powerful when they begin to affect the vision and perspective of those who do not necessarily associate themselves with those movements. So that the radical feminisms, or radical antiracist feminisms are important in the sense that they have affected the ways especially young people think about social justice struggles today.
>
> (Davis, 2016: 47)

It is with such broader levels of connectedness and solidarity across difference that progressive change can compound. Moreover, in relation to the themes in this book, it also shows how the movement of assembled bodies as a collective ethico-politics becomes a viable form of organizing for intersectional struggle which recognizes the intersectional diversity of bodies but focuses on the site of struggle to envisage change. As such, corporeal ethics distributed through assembled bodies motivates 'democratic struggles against racial, patriarchal, and economic domination' where 'the respect for otherness is a necessary condition of solidarity and democratic community' (Ziarek, 2001: 221, 224). Such is the democratic power of collective, organizing bodies in solidarity.

Networked solidarity

As we have explored above, assembled democratic political action can be understood as the emergence of corporeal ethics in a social form. This is a shared responsibility towards collective recognition and emancipation in solidarity with others. The centrality of solidarity in political resistance is explained by José Medina (2013) as follows:

> It is in and through resistance that relations of solidarity against domination and across different forms of oppression become possible and effective. Justice only becomes possible if we think through such resistance. Resistance presents as possible when we understand our own self-knowledge in working through these power relations in striving for democracy and social justice.
>
> (p. 21)

Reflecting on our positionality and relationality as social agents in networks of power relations, Medina argues that 'new possibilities of social relationality' can be garnered 'in and through resistance'. It is on account of the valuing of solidarity that Medina asks whether 'all subjects have the obligation to resist?' (p. 16). Moreover, democratic sensibilities serve to 'cultivate a resistant imagination' and a 'conception of network solidarity grounded in a kaleidoscopic social imagination, arguing that makes us sensitive to symbolic exclusions, expressive harms, and epistemic mistreatments' (p. 26). This idea of network solidarity, that Medina develops from the work of Carol Gould (2007), is key. For Gould solidarity is not limited to identification with a cohesive group. In the context of globalization and internet-based communication connections between people are broader and more diffuse. This enables new forms of solidarity and new forms of democratic relations and interactions. Built of affective relations rather than direct identification, the resulting solidarity networks can engage in the struggle for justice and human rights in a powerful way. With solidarity, Gould argues, care becomes extended to solidarity between social and political groups through 'social empathy' (p. 149). Gould's transnational networked solidarities are not an abstract idea of a common humanity, but built out of real connections between real people fighting real struggles.

The idea and practice of transnational networked solidarity enable us to think of corporeal ethics as being collectively mobilized on a global scale. Beyond the limits of caring only about those with whom one has a shared identity, this affectively grounded solidarity does not dispense with people's differences. Rather, it is achieved:

> through relations that preserve differences, that is through the construction of networks of heterogenous elements. Networks of solidarity are formed by weaving together problems, values, and

goals that, though often irreducibly different, can overlap, converge, or simply be coordinated so that they can be addressed simultaneously and enjoy mutual support.

(Medina, 2013: 308)

For us, this means that an ethical sensibility that is embodied and directed towards a radical solidarity based on overlapping political and democratic concerns marks the full potential of corporeal ethics for social justice on a global level.

Present in networked solidarity is what the Care Collective (2020) refers to as a politics of interdependence. In their Care Manifesto they offer a queer, feminist, anti-racist, eco-socialist political vision of 'universal care' that recognizes and reverses the systemic carelessness that are present in social hierarchies. Acknowledging that neoliberal authoritarianism was strengthened through the COVID-19 crisis, they describe an affective care-based politics that is increasingly essential. The manifesto argues for an interdependence of care that recognizes people's common vulnerability and our interdependence. As the Care Collective clearly articulate, organizing for universal care involves:

hands on care work, caring about and flourishing with others and the planet, collective and communal life, alternatives to capitalist markets, reversing the marketization of care infrastructures, restoring welfare states, more porous borders, Green New Deals at transnational levels, creating caring institutional institutions, cultivating every cosmopolitanism.

(p. 96)

This is a movement of collective corporeality that organizes affect in the name of care for all.

Closing

We completed writing this book in the second Sydney COVID-19 in July 2021. This was a time to reflect on how global inequalities have perpetuated if not expanded at the time of this crisis, as well as making the precarity of life feel deeper for all of us. Access to life itself is unequally distributed, with market rationalities being central to deciding 'whose health and life should be protected and whose health and life should not' (Butler, 2015: 11). As we conclude this book we think of the global violence and grief experienced by communities whose existence has been threatened. In Australia precarity is rife as people suffer at the hands of border controls with refugee families housed in detention centres which limit freedom of movement, and remote Indigenous communities affected by lack of public health. We witness the failure of nation states to protect the most vulnerable.

In *Precarious Life*, Judith Butler (2004b) reminds us that our life depends on others whom we do not know,

> our political and ethical responsibilities are rooted in the recognition that radical forms of self-sufficiency and unbridled sovereignty are, by definition, disrupted by the larger global processes of which they are a part, that no final control can be secured, and that final control is not, cannot be, an ultimate value.

(p. xiii)

Through assembly and networked solidarity the ethical and political possibility for recognition in the face of the other holds the power to produce such disruption. Corporeal ethics is not a matter of theoretical abstraction. It is the means through which life becomes worth living. It requires us to appear, and it requires a collective appearing that can create a rhythm against violent oppressive forces which continue to dominate bodies, and towards a public body which protects the most precarious and vulnerable first.

References

Arruzza, C., Bhattacharya, T., and Fraser, N. (2019) *Feminism for the 99%*. London: Verso.

Butler, J. (2004a) *Undoing Gender*. New York: Routledge.

Butler, J. (2004b) *Precarious Life: The Powers of Mourning and Violence*. London: Verso.

Butler, J. (2005) *Giving an Account of Oneself*. New York: Fordham University Press.

Butler, J. (2015) *Notes toward a Performative Theory of Assembly*. Cambridge: Harvard University Press.

Butler, J. (2016) Trump is emancipating unbridled hatred, *Zeit Online*, 28 October. Online: https://www.zeit.de/kultur/2016-10/judith-butler-donald-trump-populism-interview/komplettansicht

Butler, J., and Athanasiou, A. (2013) *Dispossession: The Performative in the Political*. Cambridge: Polity.

Care Collective. (2020) *The Care Manifesto: The Politics of Compassion*. London: Verso.

Davis, A.Y. (2016) *Freedom Is a Constant Struggle: Ferguson, Palestine, and the Foundations of a Movement*. Chicago, IL: Haymarket Books.

Fotaki, M., and Daskalaki, M. (2020). Politicizing the body in the anti-mining protest in Greece. *Organization Studies*, https://doi.org/10.1177/0170840619 882955

Gould, C.C. (2007) Transnational solidarities. *Journal of Social Philosophy*, 38(1): 148–164.

hooks, b. (1981) *Ain't I a Woman Black Women and Feminism*. London: Pluto Press.

Lloyd, M.N. (2015) *Butler and Ethics*. Edinburgh: Edinburgh University Press.

Medina, J. (2013) *The Epistemology of Resistance: Gender and Racial Oppression, Epistemic Injustice, and Resistant Imaginations*. Oxford: Oxford University Press.

Mouffe, C. (1996) *Dimensions of Radical Democracy: Pluralism, Citizenship, Community*. London: Verso.

Munro, I. (2014) Organizational ethics and Foucault's 'art of living': Lessons from social movement organizations. *Organization Studies*, 35(8): 1127–1148.

Rhodes, C. (2016) Democratic business ethics: Volkswagen's emissions scandal and the disruption of corporate sovereignty. *Organization Studies*, 37(10): 1501–1518.

Rhodes, C., Munro, I., Thanem, T., and Pullen, A. (2020) Dissensus! Radical democracy and business ethics. *Journal of Business Ethics*, 164: 627–632.

Robbins, J.W. (2011) *Radical Democracy and Political Theology*. New York: Columbia.

Thomassen, L. (2010) Radical democracy. In R. Braidotti (Ed.), pp. 169–186, *After Poststructuralism: Transitions and Transformation*. Durham: Acumen.

Tyler, M. (2019) *Judith Butler and Organization Theory*. London: Routledge.

Vachhani, S.J. (2020) Envisioning a democratic culture of difference: Feminist ethics and the politics of dissent in social movements. *Journal of Business Ethics*, 164(4): 745–757.

Young, I.M. (1990) *Throwing Like a Girl*. Bloomington: Indiana Press.

Young, I.M. (2005) *On Female Body Experience: 'Throwing Like a Girl' and Other Essays*. Oxford: Oxford University Press.

Ziarek, E.P. (2001) *An Ethics of Dissensus: Postmodernity, Feminism, and the Politics of Radical Democracy*. Stanford, CA: Stanford University Press.

Index